THE COMPLETE ODES
AND EPODES

HORACE was born in 65 BC. In 44 BC Julius Caesar was assassinated
by conspirators led by Brutus and Cassius. Two years later, when
they were defeated at Philippi, Horace commanded one of their
legions. On his return to Rome he purchased a position in the
Treasury and wrote satires and epodes under the patronage of
Maecenas, chief adviser of Octavian. With the defeat of Antony and
Cleopatra at Actium in 31 BC Octavian became master of the world,
taking the name Augustus in 27 BC. Horace *Odes* (23 BC) and Virgil's
Aeneid (19 BC) were Augustan masterpieces to rival the great
achievements of Greek poetry. Virgil died in 19 BC and two years
later Horace composed the hymn for the Secular Games, held ap-
proximately every 110 years, seeing this commission as recognition
for his life's work. In 13 BC he produced his fourth Book of Odes,
largely inspired by Pindar, the most daring and sublime of the Greek
lyric poets. He died in 8 BC, 59 days after his friend Maecenas.

DAVID WEST is Emeritus Professor of Latin in the University of
Newcastle upon Tyne. His previous publications include *Reading
Horace* (1967), *The Imagery and Poetry of Lucretius* (1969), *Virgil
Aeneid, a New Prose Translation* (1990), and *Carpe Diem* (1995), an
edition of Horace *Odes I* with translation and commentary. Similar
editions of *Odes II* and *III* are in preparation.

OXFORD WORLD'S CLASSICS

For over 100 years Oxford World's Classics have brought readers closer to the world's great literature. Now with over 700 titles—from the 4,000-year-old myths of Mesopotamia to the twentieth century's greatest novels—the series makes available lesser-known as well as celebrated writing.

The pocket-sized hardbacks of the early years contained introductions by Virginia Woolf, T. S. Eliot, Graham Greene, and other literary figures which enriched the experience of reading. Today the series is recognized for its fine scholarship and reliability in texts that span world literature, drama and poetry, religion, philosophy and politics. Each edition includes perceptive commentary and essential background information to meet the changing needs of readers.

OXFORD WORLD'S CLASSICS

HORACE

The Complete Odes and Epodes

Translated with an Introduction and Notes by
DAVID WEST

OXFORD
UNIVERSITY PRESS

OXFORD

UNIVERSITY PRESS

Great Clarendon Street, Oxford OX2 6DP

Oxford University Press is a department of the University of Oxford.
It furthers the University's objective of excellence in research, scholarship,
and education by publishing worldwide in

Oxford New York

Auckland Bangkok Buenos Aires Cape Town Chennai
Dar es Salaam Delhi Hong Kong Istanbul Karachi Kolkata
Kuala Lumpur Madrid Melbourne Mexico City Mumbai Nairobi
São Paulo Shanghai Taipei Tokyo Toronto

Oxford is a registered trade mark of Oxford University Press
in the UK and in certain other countries

Published in the United States
by Oxford University Press Inc., New York

First published as a World's Classics paperback 1997
Reissued as an Oxford World's Classics paperback 2000
Reissued 2008

British Library Cataloguing in Publication Data

Data available

Library of Congress Cataloging in Publication Data

Horace.
[Carmina. English & Latin]
The complete odes and epodes/Horace; translated with an
introduction and notes by David West.
(Oxford world's classics)
Includes bibliographical references (p.) and index.
1. Horace—Translations into English. 2. Laudatory poetry, Latin—
Translations into English. 3. Verse satire, Latin—Translations
into English. 4. Rome—Poetry. I. West, David Alexander.
II. Horace. Epodae. English & Latin. III. Title. IV. Series.
PA6395.W3913 1997 871'.01—dc21 96–43636

ISBN 978-0-19-955527-7

14

Printed and bound in Great Britain by Clays Ltd, Elcograf S.p.A.

CONTENTS

ACKNOWLEDGEMENTS

MUCH of the work for this translation was done with the help of a Leverhulme Emeritus Fellowship.

INTRODUCTION

The hazards of war landed me among the crags of occupied Crete with a band of Cretan guerrillas and a captive German general whom we had waylaid and carried off into the mountains three days before. The German garrison of the island were in hot, but luckily temporarily misdirected chase. It was a time of anxiety and danger; and for our captive, of hardship and distress. During a lull in the pursuit, we woke up among the rocks just as a brilliant dawn was breaking over the crests of Mount Ida. We had been toiling over it, through snow and then rain, for the last two days. Looking across the valley at this flashing mountain-crest, the general murmured to himself:

> vides ut alta stet nive candida
> Soracte . . .

It was one of the ones I knew! [it is *Odes* I. ix] I continued from where he had broken off:

> nec iam sustineant onus
> silvae laborantes, geluque
> flumina constiterint acuto,

and so on through the remaining five stanzas to the end. The general's blue eyes had swivelled away from the mountain-top to mine—and when I'd finished, after a long silence, he said: 'Ach so, Herr Major!' It was very strange. As though, for a long moment, the war had ceased to exist. We had both drunk at the same fountains long before.

(Patrick Leigh Fermor, 'A Time of Gifts')

THOSE who know Horace well find that of all dead writers there is none who is a closer friend, who speaks more usefully in easy and in difficult times, and none whom they would more happily sit down to drink with. Those who know him less well may argue that the character he presents is an ingratiating artefact, trading in false modesty, self-mockery, superficial wordly wisdom, an 'English' sense of humour, a toadying to the regime which had enriched him, a convoluted word order and a sequence of thought like Stephen Leacock's Lord Ronald, who flung himself upon his horse and rode madly off in all directions. But lovers of the man know all this and smile, answering simply that Horace knew it too.

The Life of Horace

Quintus Horatius Flaccus was born in 65 BC in Venusia, a town near where Lucania and Apulia met in central south Italy. His father was an auctioneer's agent, owned a small farm, and was a freedman, that is a slave who had been freed in his lifetime. He took a great interest in his son's education, taking him to Rome to study Greek, and sending him to Athens, where his principal study was Greek philosophy. On the Ides of March 44 BC Julius Caesar had been assassinated by conspirators led by Brutus and Cassius. Brutus then withdrew to Athens and, while attending lectures in philosophy and gathering an army, he recruited young Horace with the rank of *tribunus militum*, the second level of legionary command under the *legatus*. After the conspirators were defeated in 42 BC by Antony and Octavian at the battle of Philippi, Horace returned to Rome and purchased an administrative post as *scriba quaestorius*, a Treasury official assisting the elected magistrates. In 38 BC he was introduced to Maecenas, friend and adviser of Octavian. Horace's first book of *Satires* appeared in 35 BC, and soon after that, thanks to the generosity of Maecenas, he became the happy owner of an estate in the Sabine hills east of Rome. In 31 BC Octavian defeated Antony and Cleopatra at the battle of Actium and in 27 BC he took the title of Augustus. The *Epodes* and a second book of *Satires* appeared in 30 BC, the first three books of *Odes* in 23, the *Epistles* in 19, the *Secular Hymn* in 17, the fourth book of *Odes* in 13 BC and about the same time the second book of *Epistles*. Maecenas died in 8 BC and in his will, by which he left all his property to Augustus, there is a clause 'Be mindful of Horatius Flaccus as though he were myself' (*Horati Flacci ut mei memor esto*). Horace died fifty-nine days later and the two men were buried close to one another on Maecenas' estate on the Esquiline Hill in Rome.

These are bare facts. It is not easy to relate them to the poetic personality which Horace fashioned from these materials. Pride in his birthplace is an important element in his poetry, as attested in his *Satire* II. i. 34–41:

> I do not know whether I am a Lucanian or an Apulian,
> since the Venusian farmer ploughs the border between the two,
> sent there, according to tradition, when the Samnites

were driven out, to make sure that Rome's enemies
could not attack over open ground
whether it was wild Apulians or Lucanians
who threatened war. But this pen of mine
will attack no living creature unless provoked.
It will protect me staying hidden in its sheath.

Horace refers to his descent from this sturdy Italian stock in many places in his lyric poetry, sometimes, as here, to insist upon his own loyalty and his own independence, sometimes to delight in the Italian landscape as in the birds' eye view of his native mountains at III. iv. 14–16, sometimes to praise the peoples of Italy as at III. vi. 37–44 and iii. 23, and often to reflect upon his achievement in coming from such a background to give the Latin language a body of poetry which can stand beside the great lyric poetry of Greece (III. xiii and xxx). It is relevant also to remember that Octavian cultivated the peoples of Italy and they were solidly in his favour. As early as 36 BC the Italian cities were putting up statues of him in their temples.

Horace's father poses a puzzle which has only recently been solved by Gordon Williams (1995). How could a freedman of modest means have afforded to take his son to school in Rome and send him to mix with the sons of the great at university in Athens? How could a freedman's son in his early twenties so impress Brutus that he was recruited to a rank which meant that he might be called upon to command a Roman legion? And how could he come back to Rome after the defeat of Brutus at Philippi and purchase an important and lucrative post in political administration?

First of all, these *facts* have to be read in the contexts in which Horace presents them, as in *Satire* I. vi. 45–52:

Now I come back to my own case, the freedman's son
whom everybody sneers at because I'm a freedman's son.
They do it now because I live with you. They did it before
because I was a tribune and had a legion under my command.
The two cases are different. People might be right
to envy my rank, but not your friendship, above all
because you recruit only those who are worthy of it
and have nothing to do with social climbers.

The poem is clearly a testament of gratitude and admiration from Horace to his father. But it is also a tribute to Horace's patron Maecenas, and its thrust is to establish the character of Maecenas by arguing that he judges men according to their merits. To increase the merits of Maecenas, Horace diminishes his own. His father's freedman status is a gibe which Horace has had to endure and which he is now turning to advantage. Further, his father's occupation as an auctioneer's agent, *coactor*, was not such a humble position as it may sound in English. The *coactor*'s role was to collect the purchase money from the bidder and transmit it to the seller. He would not have failed to take his percentage. In these troubled times where rich properties were being confiscated and booty coming on the market, great fortunes were made by agents as well as auctioneers. But the essence of the argument rests upon a reconstruction of the history of Venusia. Venusia was the only Latin colony to join the allies of Rome who rose against her in the Social War of 91–88. It was stormed by the Romans in 88 BC and more than 3,000 prisoners were taken. *If*—and Gordon Williams admits that this is only a hypothesis—Horace's grandfather and father were among those captured, there are parallels which suggest that they might have been sold as slaves. After the Social War Roman citizenship was granted to the peoples of Italy, but before this could be taken up those who had been captured and enslaved would have had to be manumitted. To call such men freedmen would be a good schoolboy's gibe, but it would be a malicious travesty of the facts. And it would not explain how Horace's father was able to give his son an education that would bring him into contact with the greatest men of Rome. The answer to the puzzle is that Horace, in spite of his own evidence, was wealthy and well connected. He was also shrewd and agreeable. And perhaps Brutus saw that he had inherited some financial acumen from his father, which would make him useful in military administration.

The *Epodes*

By and large Latin poets did not invent new forms, but accepted types of poems and the elements and characteristics appropriate to each type, from the works of their Greek predecessors. Within this discipline arose the colossal explosion of creative energy in the poetry of Plautus and Terence, Catullus and Lucretius, Horace and Virgil, to name but six.

Horace tells us at *Epistles* I. xix. 23–5 that he followed the metres and the spirit of Archilochus, the Greek poet who had lived seven centuries before him on the island of Paros. The metres of the surviving *Epodes* of Archilochus consist of shorter lines alternating with longer in the iambic metre (like Horace *Epodes* i–x), but the iambics are sometimes used in combination with various patterns of dactylic rhythms (like Horace, *Epodes* xi–xvi). None of the surviving poems of Archilochus is written in iambic lines of the same length (like Horace *Epode* xvii).

The fragments of Archilochus' *Epodes* are too scanty to give us an impression of their content, but the Archilochian spirit in general is well known. He was a soldier and he wrote of poems of war, wine, and love, strikingly robust in tone, and was famous for his poems of violent abuse, so much so that the word *iambs* in Latin and Greek denotes poems of invective. So Horace's *Epodes* include poems of war, of which i and ix present the relationships between men engaged in battle, and vii and xvi are addresses to the people. There are four convivial poems (i, iii, ix, xiii), robust poems of love (xi, xiv, xv), and poems of abuse: cheerful, such as iii; violent, such as iv, vi, x; or vicious, such as the denunciations of old women in viii and xii and of witches in v and xvii. This leaves the most famous of all the *Epodes*, the praise of the ideal country life in ii, whose cynical last four lines qualify the poem for the genre but puzzle the reader. The best explanation is that the poem, like the first and the third, is written in honour of his patron Maecenas, in particular for his gift to Horace of the Sabine farm. In this interpretation the sting in the tail is a smiling device to remove from the poem any flavour of flattery or subservience.

These poems are sometimes explained in terms of Horace's own experience of life, as expressions of the bitterness he must have known after the battle of Philippi where his ambition, his importance, and his republican ideals ended in defeat. This view is surely wrong. The poems appeared in 30 BC and as early as 38 BC his past was forgiven and he was accepted into the inner circle of the poets round Maecenas, who was the close confidant of

Octavian and one of the most important men in Rome. Instead of finding with some scholars a sensibility irritated by hardship and bitterness, it might be more revealing to examine how the *Epodes* fit into the policies and ideology of Octavian and his supporters in the thirties BC.

There is no doubt that from his first entry into politics Octavian was consciously engaged in manipulating public opinion. This is vividly demonstrated by Du Quesnay on page 22 of his study of the first book of the *Satires*, which starts from the following premiss: 'The task facing the young Octavian, if he was to avoid the fate of Julius Caesar, is simply defined. He had to build upon his hard-won success, to increase his real power and his reputation without seeming to be a tyrant, and to increase and broaden the basis of his support.' This was achieved by presenting his political aspirations as being the restoration of peace, law and order, and prosperity, after a century of civil war and social turmoil. Further, in later life, Octavian, now called Augustus, was to boast that he had found Rome brick and left it marble, and even in the thirties the seeds of that ambition must have been germinating. His life's work was to create the greatest empire and the noblest city that man had ever seen, and towards that programme he was also, with the aid of Maecenas, to preside over a moral and religious reformation. A cultural renaissance or naissance was a plank in that programme. His involvement was personal. He gave every possible encouragement to men of talent of his age, going so far as to listen to them reading their poems and histories, even their speeches and dialogues (Suetonius, *Life of Augustus* 89). The effect of the first book of the *Satires* was to present Maecenas and his friends as humane, humorous, cultured, morally serious, and above all flattery and corruption. Maecenas himself was a sophisticated Epicurean. When Brutus and Cassius sank their daggers in the body of Julius Caesar, their watchword was *Libertas*, and all the contestants in the wars that followed claimed to be fighting for Liberty. The liberty offered by Octavian included personal liberty to enjoy the good things of life. All this is amply documented for the thirties BC in the revealing study by Du Quesnay, and the *Epodes* were written in the thirties. In this aspect of the policies of Augustus as they were later to develop, a constant spur would be the glory of

Greece. Virgil's *Aeneid* would be greeted by Propertius (*Elegies* II. xxxiv. 66) in about 23 BC as something greater than Homer's *Iliad*, but even before this claim Octavian would surely have been receptive to a work of poetic promise giving Rome its own Archilochus, produced by a young poet in the entourage of his chief adviser. The Archilochian *Epodes* of Horace are therefore proto-Augustan in that they create Roman poetry that can stand beside the Greek.

In detail, the war poems listed above celebrate the battle of Actium from the point of view of men engaged in it. The addresses to the Roman people in *Epodes* vii and xvi chime with the moral tone of later Augustan literature including Horace's own *Odes*. The love poems are acceptable to the Epicurean approach to love which approved sexual activity but rejected sexual infatuation. Meanwhile, Antony was indulging in his sexual infatuation with Cleopatra, a prime target for Octavian's propaganda, and by the late thirties Tibullus and Propertius were beginning to write elegies of unhappy love, based on a way of life not unlike that of Antony but very un-Epicurean, and very un-Augustan. Most illuminating and important for the relationship between Horace and his patron and for the political as well as personal interpretation of these poems is the third epode, the squib which ends with a dire curse upon Maecenas if he serves Horace a dish with too much garlic in it. These men, Horace, Maecenas, and Augustus, conversed in an unbuttoned style, as demonstrated most clearly in the letters of Augustus himself quoted by Suetonius in his *Life of Horace*, translated following this Introduction. The rough badinage speaks of conviviality, trust, and cheerful fun. So to demonstrate the tolerance, humour, and humanity of the new leaders of Rome, as Horace has already done in the first book of the *Satires*, is a political act. In this respect too, these *Epodes* are proto-Augustan poems.

Furthermore, the poems of abuse establish the Archilochian status of this new poetry, which, as argued above, is in accord with the cultural vision of the new Rome as the rival of Greece. The praise of country life in the second epode would have been acceptable to Octavian in his role as saviour and friend of the people of Italy, and Virgil's *Georgics* is surely associated with the same policy. True, the acidic ending of the poem makes it difficult to interpret, but no doubt the sting in the tail is a concession to the Archilochian spirit which Horace is imitating. This leaves the witches in *Epodes* v and xvii. In this matter it may be important to remember that Maecenas had bought land on the Esquiline Hill, which was a squalid haunt of magicians, witches, and low life, and built here his famous palace, tower, and gardens. It would be typical of the art of oblique praise as practised by Horace to celebrate at v. 100 and xvii. 58 and also in *Satire* I. viii. 14 this reclamation and this glorious estate, which would fall into place as part of the Augustan beautification of Rome, by poems denouncing and mocking the superstitious practices which Maecenas had put an end to. It would be typical of Horace to praise the palace of Maecenas without mentioning it.

Odes, Books I–III (23 BC)

In the twenties BC the man found his time and his task. Rome had conquered the world, but Rome knew that it was no match in literary culture for the great age of Greece. Virgil was working on a Roman *Iliad* to rival the epics of Homer; Horace, for his part, tried to produce Latin poetry to rival the lyric poets of Greece, notably Alcaeus, Pindar, Sappho, and Anacreon. To trace Horace's loving use of this poetry, the great commentaries on the first two books of *Odes* by Nisbet and Hubbard are essential.

In the three books of *Odes* which appeared in 23 BC Horace, like his Greek predecessors, dealt with politics and war, with wine, friendship, love, and death, with poetry, music, and the gods. No longer does his verse rattle along in an iambic te-tum te-tum te-tum. It now deploys a wide range of metres adapted for Latin from Greek lyric poetry, which it would be foolish for an English translator to try to reproduce. To set out his stall Horace writes each of the first nine odes of the first book in a different metre. These Parade Odes, as they have been called, give a fair sample also of the range of his subject matter and style, and we shall now use them as Horace did, to introduce these astonishing poems.

The first ode gives a sharply observed account of other men's enthusiasms, constructed as a comparison of different lives, a form familiar in Greek and Latin literature (see below on the fourth ode). All these interests of men are gently and genially mocked, including Horace's own, showing that the poet is the same as the rest of us, and different from the rest of us. The Olympic victor wears a crown of palm leaves and is raised to the gods; Horace, too, is raised to the gods but wears a crown of ivy. The electoral candidate is raised by the people of Rome; Horace hopes to be raised by the judgement of his patron Maecenas. The soldier thrills to trumpet and bugle; Horace craves the pipe and the lyre. The huntsman leaves his lovely wife and stays out all the cold night long; Horace stays away from people in the cool woods with Nymphs and Satyrs. He is serious about his calling, but not pompous, and that attitude runs through his poems about poetry, notably I. xxxi, II. xix and xx, III. xxv. Horace ends by stating his ambition to be ranked with the lyric poets of Greece. The lyre of Lesbos points to the songs of the two great poets of that island in the seventh and sixth century BC, Sappho and Alcaeus, the latter of whom inspires more of Horace's odes than does any other poet. The reference to the pipe suggests the music which would have accompanied the mighty choral odes of Pindar, the Boeotian poet of the sixth century BC, famous for his daring imagery, his great rolling periods, his leaps of sense, his lofty moral reflections and mythological paradigms. *Odes* IV. ii, iv, and xiv are striking examples.

The second ode is a poem in praise of Augustus. Like Virgil, Horace is a praise poet, and like Virgil he realized that praise must not too often be explicit, but should rather proceed by indirection. Here, for instance, he praises Augustus with reference to his family, the *Julian* family which took its name from Aeneas' son, Ascanius Iulus, once known as Ilus. The ode starts with a surrealistic description of a flood which is three floods. First it is a flood raised by Tiber to protest against the rape by Mars of the Trojan priestess *Ilia* who is now his wife; secondly it is a flood which recalls the famous prodigies, including a flood

(Virgil *Georgic* I. 482–3), which occurred on the assassination of *Julius* Caesar in 44 BC; thirdly, it alludes to the flood of the Tiber on the night of 16 January 27 BC, three days after Augustus, adopted son of *Julius*, caused consternation by threatening to give up office and return to private life. The poem ends with a hymn calling upon a god to come and save Rome, and, like the comparison of lives in the first ode, it exploits an established form. The ancient hymn often included a list of different names for the god in the hope that one of them would be persuasive. Here Horace calls upon Apollo, who gave Octavian/Augustus the victory at Actium, or Venus, the mother of the *Julians*, or Mars, the father of Romulus by *Ilia*, or 'if Mercury is here in the guise of Augustus, let him stay with us for many long years, and not be whisked up to the sky' like Romulus, his *Julian* forebear. Scholars have sometimes said baldly that Horace here deifies Augustus. Not so. By a sleight of syntax, he has played with an old formula to praise Augustus and stopped just short of direct statement and blatant flattery. The battle of Actium made Augustus the most powerful man in the Mediterranean world. In the early twenties Maecenas was his chief minister, and Maecenas was the patron of Horace. Praise of the Augustan achievement appears throughout the *Odes*, notably in the sequence of six 'Roman Odes' which begins the third book, and frequently in the fourth.

The third ode is addressed to Horace's friend Virgil, the other great poet of the Augustan regime, who introduced him to Maecenas and thence to the circle of Octavian/Augustus. It condemns the boldness and ambition of men, and ends with a reference to the lightning of Jupiter, which appears later in the *Odes* as the god's armoury in the battle of the Gods and Giants, which in turn, notably in III. iv, is seen as an analogy for the war in which Octavian/Augustus defeated Antony and Cleopatra. The lightning of Jupiter is part of the armoury of Augustus.

The odes of Horace are almost all—I. xxxiv is an exception—addressed to named individuals. The mythological allusion here, and the serious reflection on the ambitions of men, would well have suited Virgil's own attitudes. In this ode a poet is addressing a poet and a friend. Virgil could read the subtext. Many of the odes are lit by a similar glow of sympathy and friendship, notably I. xxiv, and all the odes addressed to Maecenas, some light-hearted, such as I. xx, some profound like III. xxix.

The fourth ode is addressed to Lucius Sestius, who had fought for Brutus against Octavian at Philippi in 42 BC, and in 23 BC when these poems appeared was appointed consul to take the place of Augustus, thus signalling the reconciliation and harmony which are part of the Augustan programme. The ode again demonstrates that Horace tends to tool his poems to his addressees, as detailed in the note on I. iv. 14. This is poetry made for the man whom it addresses, *ad hominem* poetry, and such personal details are again and again revealingly expounded by Nisbet and Hubbard, particularly in their commentary on the second book.

The fifth ode is a poem about love, a farewell to a demanding, fickle, and temperamental mistress, in effect to love as depicted by the contemporary elegiac poets Tibullus and Propertius. The mysterious power of this poem stems largely from the resonance of the metaphor that runs through it. Pyrrha is a sea, now smiling, but soon dangerous. G. B. Conte, the doyen of writers on literary theory in Latin poetry, wrote in 1994 on page 311 of his 'Latin Literature: A History', translated by J. B. Solodow, of Horace's 'cautious employment of metaphors and similes'. But Horace is one of the three great virtuosi of metaphor in Latin poetry, falling short of the monstrous fertility of Plautus and the sublimity of Lucretius, but unique in complex ways which can only be called Horatian. This vivid poetic gift illumines almost all his odes.

   The love poems of Horace raise an important problem. Although he reacted against 'elegiac love' and makes fun of it, he himself wrote many love poems. But Horatian love is not tempestuous and agonized. It is more of an Epicurean love, a compact of affection, good humour, and shared pleasures, including in Horace the pleasures of wine and music. This perhaps goes some way towards explaining why some readers think that Horace wrote great love poems and many believe that he wrote no love poems at all. Another problem arises from the large number of names in the roll-call of his ladies—Pyrrha, Leuconoe, Lydia, Tyndaris, Glycera, and Chloe in the first book of odes alone. Yet the serious political odes are loud in support of Augustus' condemnation of adultery and sexual licence. Part of an explanation may be that the Augustan cultural programme welcomed lyric poetry in Latin to rival the lyric poetry of Greece. Such love poems were part of the Greek tradition. Therefore, the Augustan programme had to welcome such love poems in Latin.

But there is a more radical approach to this problem. To ask whether Horace approved of promiscuity or fidelity is absurd. Poets are not on oath, nor are they required to address ethical or philosophical questions, to provide evidence before a court or contributions to serious debate. The question is not whether Horace loved the Lyde of III. xxviii or the Phyllis of IV. xi, or, if he did, whether that love was profound or shallow, genuine or exploitative, or whether Lyde or Phyllis or comparable females differently named ever existed, or whether Horace ever made love to woman or boy. We have no information at all on any of these questions. What we have is the poems and these stand or fall for other reasons, which include the quality of the life they represent, but not its evidential status. So III. vi is a denunciation of adultery and III. vii is an amusing squib on the same topic. Augustus clearly appreciated the first, and equally clearly did not think that its message was diluted by the frivolity of the second or by the large number of lovers mentioned in Horace's poetry.

The sixth of these Parade Odes, like the first and the second, demonstrates Horace's way of taking a formula and making it unique. In the *recusatio* (see introductory note on this poem) the poet protests his inability to rise to the heights required worthily to praise his patron. He then suggests the name of some other poet who could so rise, then either demonstrates his own incompetence, or else shows in a flash that he can do it perfectly well himself, and finally gives a low-key account of his own modest literary programme. Two are therefore praised in one poem, here Augustus' great general Agrippa, and Varius, the greatest dramatist of the day and a favourite of Augustus. Besides, Horace has had some fun. Such is the *recusatio*—the unkind might call it a formula for the production of poems—but in Horace's hands the formula gives freedom to innovate and aston-ish, as demonstrated in each of the first two odes in the fourth book.

The seventh ode is a variation on yet another formula, the *priamel*, of which we have already seen an example in the first poem. This consists of a list of activities or desires, followed by a declaration of the preference of the poet. Sappho (fragment 16) gives a defining example:

> Some say that an army of horsemen
> is the most beautiful thing upon the black earth,
> others an army of foot soldiers or a fleet of ships,
>   but for me it is whatever one loves.

Here in the seventh ode the *priamel* form is used to praise yet another lieutenant of Antony's, who defected to Octavian when Antony allowed Cleopatra to come with him on the cam-paign which led to the battle of Actium. Again, as in I. iv, a Parade Ode is used to demonstrate Augustan clemency and reconciliation.

The eighth ode is another love poem, in which Horace expostu-lates with a Lydia who has lured a young Sybaris from his military training on the Campus Martius. Clearly Sybaris, des-pite the Greek name, is a pseudonym for a young Roman. Not that any particular Roman boy is in Horace's sights. These are Latin poems in the manner of Greek lyric. To associate a Roman with such activities would be demeaning, and to give the charac-ter a Roman name would be prosaic. This is a poem about contemporary Rome, and contemporary anywhere. The Greek name makes it a cultural coup for Augustan Rome, perhaps not unlike Chloris, Clorinda, and Delia in the love poems of Robert Burns. Horace, now in his early forties, is committed by his literary programme to write of love and wine. But his friends, distinguished and dignified Romans, might not be pleased to appear in such scenes. Horace solves the problem by finding a role for himself as a worldly-wise, sophisticated friend, adviser, and gentle mocker of the young, the Professor of Love,

Praeceptor Amoris, very like Don Alfonso in Mozart's *Così fan tutte*. He plays this role, for example, at I. xxvii and xxix.

The ninth ode is the Soracte Ode with which this Introduction began. It marks the passage of Thaliarchus from boyhood and the love of Horace, to manhood and the love of girls. This is not to say that Horace was a practising homosexual. To repeat the arguments put forward on the fifth ode, we do not know anything about his sexual tastes or practices. These are poems, not clinical reports, and not evidence for the life of their author. In this context, 'Horace' means 'the persona presented by the poet in the poem'. That persona is a poetic construct and there is no way of getting behind it. Homosexual poems are part of the Greek tradition and Horace follows it at the end of I. iv, for example, and in I. xxix, I, xxxviii and IV. xii. Whether he ever had a boy lover, we do not know and never shall.

This ode gives an example of a Horatian device. Its opening closely resembles the opening of a Greek poem, in this case by Alcaeus: 'Zeus is sending rain, there is a great storm from heaven, and the water of the rivers is frozen . . . Down with the storm. Stoke up the fire, and mix the honey-sweet wine.' There are several of these 'motto' poems (I. xii from Pindar, I. xvi from Stesichorus, I. xviii and xxxvii from Alcaeus) and no doubt more whose Greek originals have not been preserved. They vividly demonstrate the debt of Horace to the Greeks, and his independence.

These first nine odes, each in a different metre, give a fair sample of the variety in Horace's lyric poetry. The next poem also demands a word. The tenth ode is a hymn to Mercury. Many Horatians look upon the gods in Horace as literary constructs, as pasteboard figures, useful for the associations they bring with them. On the other hand, it may be felt that Horace loved his gods, and sensed their presence, Apollo for example, for his sweet reason and his gift of music and poetry. This does not necessarily mean that Apollo is an allegory or a symbol. The god can be present as a god, as Apollo and Bacchus are when Horace is composing, as Venus is in the mystery of love, as Mercury is in this glorious poem. Horace is a Mercury man *Mercurialis vir*,

(II. xvii. 29) and here he contemplates Mercury's contribution to human life—civilization and humane activities, music, fun, mischief, protection in danger, and joy after death. The gods in Horace, on this interpretation, are not abstract concepts or allegories. They actually visit him, in their traditional garb with their traditional character and iconography, at those moments when he senses the arrival of something supernatural in the flow of his life. Striking examples are in I. xix, xxvi, xxx, xxxi, xxxii.

The Secular Hymn and *Odes* IV

Virgil having died in 19 BC, it was Horace, in his fiftieth year, in 17 BC, who was commissioned to produce a hymn for the Secular Festival to celebrate the achievements of the Augustan regime. The performance of this *Carmen Saeculare* at the greatest festival Rome had ever seen was the supreme accolade for the career of Horace as a poet. His pride in this recognition shines through in the fourth book he produced to celebrate the victories of Augustus' young relatives in wars in Gaul and Germany. One of the factors that saves this political poetry from the hazards that attend panegyric is its daring experiments in the Pindaric style (see above, p. xv). Horace decided that Pindar was the target which a lyric poet must aim at, and he aimed. Poetry of patronage is not necessarily contemptible if the poet believes (Bach and Haydn might be cited as examples). At first reading the Secular Hymn and the fourth book of *Odes* are far from modern taste and difficult to take, but those who persevere in hope may come to see them as some of the precious life-blood of a master spirit—not that Horace would ever say such a thing.

The personal poems in this fourth book are full of Horace's sense of the passing of time. He knew that love and friends and conviviality were slipping from his grasp. He says so in 19 BC in *Epistles* I. vii. 25–7:

Give me back my manly vigour, my black hair and unreceded brow,
give me back the sweetness in my voice, my musical laugh,
the grief I knew in my cups when the delicious Cinara left me.

Here in his farewell to lyric poetry he speaks as usefully as
anyone can about such matters as love and death. The end of IV.
xi catches the tone:

> age, iam, meorum
>   finis amorum
> —non enim posthac alia calebo
> femina—

> Come then, last of my loves
> —for after this I shall never warm to any other woman—

This brief survey has given a view of the sweep of Horace's
lyric poetry. We have seen that these poems are a continuation of
the great lyric poetry of Greece, and that they often signal their
debt, particularly to Alcaeus and Pindar. They use the estab-
lished formulas of Greek poetry: hymn, *priamel*, *recusatio*,
mythological paradigm. Horace was steeped in things Greek—
but whatever he took he made his own. Greek philosophy lies
behind the pervasive Epicureanism, the Stoicism, for instance of
II. ii, and Horace's own elusive thinking in III. xxix. Later Greek
poetry, notably the Palatine Anthology, is the inspiration for
many poems—invitations and dedications, and poems of love
and wine. We have seen glimpses of his humour and studied his
tactical deftness as a client poet. His poetry is steeped also in the
affairs of the day. He is interested in those he addresses and
sensitive and affectionate towards his friends. He has an eye for
metaphor and a taste for the surreal. But this catalogue does not
catch the essence of the Horatian ode. This is partly because of
his diversity. In the seventeenth century the Royalist James
Shirley was moved to imitate his sublime eloquence, Andrew
Marvell to grave and profound reflection on the affairs of his own
time and the evils of tyranny, Robert Herrick to poems of sunlit
delicacy. There is no simple formula for a Horatian ode, but
there are some striking characteristics not yet mentioned. The
sound is unique, setting against elaborate, fixed metres the music
of powerful speech. The complexity of the structure of many of
the poems amazes with subtle transitions, astonishing leaps
of sense, and rich modulations of feeling. The elusiveness of
Horace is familiar. Every reader seems to find his own Horace.
Jeremiah Markland, the great English eighteenth-century classi-

cal scholar, admitted that with a lifetime of effort he could not understand a single ode of Horace. The diversity of his subject matter makes him a poet for many human situations, from love, for example, to the loss of love.

But a salient characteristic is the lapidary brevity of the language. This perhaps explains why Virgil, who is commonly held to be the greatest of the Roman poets, fills about half of Horace's column-inches in most dictionaries of quotations. It is a complex alchemy. Consider four famous tags. In I. iii *Nil mortalibus ardui est*, translated in *The Oxford Book of Quotations* 'No height is too arduous for mortal men'. But *ardui* is not only 'arduous'. It is also 'steep', and the whole of this phrase leaps into richer sense when read in its context in the ode. Horace is much richer when the literal meaning of words is not forgotten. Or take Pyrrha in the fifth ode, *simplex munditiis*, 'plain in thy neatness', as translated by John Milton. But *simplex* hints at simplicity and truth, and *munditiis* at cleanliness, elegance, style. The two words are totally beyond the reach of translation. Or take *carpe diem* in I. xi, 'Snatch the sleeve of today', as translated in *The Oxford Book of Quotations*. But Horace is telling Leuconoe to cut back long hopes to a short space, to strain the wine, to *pluck the day* and leave as little as possible for tomorrow. 'The day' is wine, pleasure, serenity, love. It is also the ripe grape. There are no sleeves. Or consider the Golden Mean in II. x. 5, *aurea mediocritas*. Nothing could be drabber and more commonplace than the mean, and nothing is rarer and more precious than gold. Nisbet and Hubbard start their commentary on the first book by saying that the odes are too familiar to be easily understood. We have to try to read them with fresh eyes to see how surreal, how paradoxical, how sharp such passages are.

A final diagnostic characteristic takes us back to where this Introduction began. Horace has a way of making some people love him. We can either say that he has invented an engaging poetic persona, or that of all dead poets there is none whose company we enjoy more.

THE LIFE OF HORACE

(believed to be an abbreviation of a Life *by Suetonius)*

Until his dismissal in 122 AD Suetonius was secretary to the Emperor Hadrian and had access to the papers of Augustus. The value of this short life is in the words of Augustus and Maecenas which it cites. These men were clearly on easy, affectionate, bantering terms with each other and with Horace. For instance, the beginning of the second paragraph shows that Augustus and Maecenas are patrons and benefactors, while Horace is client and recipient, but all three are friends, and Augustus can joke about their relationship. A parasite in Greek is one who eats at a great man's table and in Latin the great man is called a king, *rex*.

Some details have to be taken with a pinch of salt. The great mystery in Horace's life is his meteoric rise from being the son of a freedman in a remote town in Apulia to sitting at lectures with the wealthiest and most aristocratic young Romans at university in Athens, and then finding himself at the age of 23 in command of a Roman legion at the battle of Philippi. This is discussed on page x of the Introduction, where it is argued that the notion that Horace's father was a freedman (that is a slave who had been freed) is a calumny which Horace reproduced as part of a strategy of self-vindication. It is more likely that he had been a prisoner of war in the Social Wars of 90–89 BC. Soon afterwards he would have been pardoned, resumed his status as a Roman citizen, and prospered, with a town house, a farm (*Epistle* II. ii. 50), and financial interests. Nor need we believe that Horace's father ever sold salt fish. Ancient biography thrived on lies about the parents of the great and Fraenkel (*Horace*, 6–7) beautifully traces the origin of this one. Even then pornography was a canonical element in the biographer's trade. We do not need to believe in the bedroom of mirrors.

QUINTUS HORATIUS FLACCUS had a freedman father, as Horace himself records, who was an auctioneer's agent, and was believed to have been a seller of salt fish—someone once said to Horace in an argument, 'How often have I seen your father wiping his nose on his arm.' In the war which ended with the battle of Philippi, he was recruited by the general Marcus Brutus and served as a military tribune. After his side was defeated, he was pardoned and purchased the office of quaestor's clerk. He then won for himself the favour first of Maecenas, and then of Augustus, and held a high place in the affections of both men. Maecenas makes it clear enough how much he loved him in this well-known epigram:

> If I do not love you now, Horace,
> more than I love my own belly,
> I'd be thinner to look at than a hinny,

but he is more eloquent in his final judgement in a codicil to his will addressed to Augustus, 'Be mindful of Horatius Flaccus as though he were myself'.

Augustus offered him the post of secretary, as is indicated by this note to Maecenas: 'Until now I have managed to write letters to my friends in my own hand, but now that I am so extremely busy and not in good health, I wish to take our Horace away from you. So then he will come from that parasite's table of yours to my royal one, and help me write my letters.' Even when Horace refused, Augustus was not at all offended and continued to cultivate his friendship. There are surviving letters from which I add some extracts to prove the point: 'Take upon yourself some rights in my house, as though you were living with me. This would be proper, since this is the relationship I have wanted with you if your health allowed it.' And again, 'How I remember you, you can find out from our friend Septimius. Even if you are so proud as to spurn our friendship, we are not for that reason going to be counterfastidious. Augustus also made jokes, calling him, for example, a very perfect penis and a very charming little man, and he made him rich by one act of generosity after another. Indeed, he so admired his writings and was so convinced that they would endure for all time, that he commissioned him not only to write the Secular Hymn but also to celebrate the victory of his stepsons Drusus and Tiberius over the Vindelici and add for this purpose a fourth book of odes a long time after the first three. Further, after he had read some of Horace's *Epistles*, he complained in these words that they made no mention of himself: 'I'd have you understand that I'm angry with you. In all your writings of this sort you speak with others but never with me. Are you afraid it will damage you with posterity if you are known to be a friend of ours?' This is how he extracted from Horace the piece beginning:

> Since you bear alone the burden of so many responsibilities,
> protecting Italy with arms, improving its morals,
> and amending its laws, it would be contrary to the public interest,
> Caesar, if I wasted your time in lengthy chatter.

In appearance he was short and fat, as described in his own *Satires* and by Augustus in this letter: 'Onysius has brought me your little book, which, small as it is, I accept in good part as your apology. You seem to me to be afraid that your books will be bigger than you are yourself, but it's height you lack; there's no shortage of bulk. You could write on a pint-pot and the circumference of your volume would have the *embonpoint* of your own paunch.'

He is said to have been exceptionally intemperate in his love affairs, and there is a story that he so disposed his lovers in a mirrored room that whichever way he looked, there was a reflection of sexual intercourse. He lived mostly in his country retreats, either on the Sabine estate or in Tibur, where his house is pointed out near the little grove of Tiburnus. There have come into my hands elegies under his name and a prose epistle in which he commends himself to Maecenas, but I think them both spurious. The elegies are trite and the letter is obscure, and obscurity is not one of his faults.

He was born in the sixth day before the Ides of December [8 December 65 BC] in the consulate of Lucius Cotta and Lucius Torquatus, and died on the fifth day before the Kalends of that same month in the consulship of Gaius Marcius Censorinus and Gaius Asinius Gallus [27 November 8 BC], in his fifty-seventh year, and fifty-nine days after the death of Maecenas. He named Augustus as his heir by word of mouth, because the onset of his illness made him incapable of signing a will. He was buried in a grave near the tomb of Maecenas on the far side of the Esquiline Hill.

TRANSLATOR'S NOTE

THE odes of Horace are among the densest lyric poems ever written. The allusions are rich and subtle, and the tone is so iridescent that readers can never be quite sure of it, and find endless pleasure in disagreeing with each other about it. Translation of poetry is always impossible but translation of Horace's odes is inconceivable. Literal versions are useful to Latin students, but bear no relation to the character and tone of the poetry. James Michie's versions are brilliant creations by a real poet, but their sheer brilliance gives them an un-Horatian veneer. What is offered here is much wordier and is not written in any regular metre, but it is closer to the Latin. It aims to give a text which enables non-Latin readers to gain some understanding of the detail of the poetry and of how it works, and to do so in English which can be read without revulsion. In the first book the translation is lightly adapted from the versions which support the commentary in my *Carpe Diem* (Oxford, 1995).

This translation divides each epode into sections to help to clarify the run of sense. There is no authority for these divisions. Most of these poems are in the iambic metre (te-tum te-tum) with a longer line alternating with a shorter. This general shape is preserved in the translation but in each poem the Latin lines, unlike the English, have a fixed number of feet. But see introductory remarks on xi and xvii in the Explanatory Notes.

Horace did not give his poems individual titles. The titles used here are the first few words of each poem in the Latin. An index of these is given at the back of the book.

NOTE ON THE TEXT

THE text translated is the Oxford Classical Text edited by
E. C. Wickham (Oxford, 1912) with some variations of which the
following, given with the numeration of the Latin text, are the
most important:

Epodes

ii. 25	rivis] ripis
ii. 27	fontes] frondes
v. 87	magnum] magica
ix. 17	ad hunc] at huc
xi. 16	ut haec . . . dividat] adhuc . . . dividam
xiii. 13	parvi] proni
xv. 15	offensae] offensi
xvii. 11	unxere] luxere

Odes, Book I

ii. 39	Mauri] Marsi
vi. 19	cantamus vacui, sive] cantamus, vacui sive
vii. 27	auspice: Teucri] auspice Teucro
viii. 2	hoc deos vere] te deos oro
viii. 4	oderit] deserit
viii. 6	equitet] equitat
viii. 7	temperet] temperat
ix. 18	campus] Campus
xii. 31	*quia] quom
xv. 20	cultus] crinis
xvii. 9	Haediliae] haediliae
xx. 5	care] clare
xxi. 8	Cragi] Gragi
xxiii. 5	veris] vepris
xxiii. 7	adventus] ad ventum
xxv. 20	Hebro] Euro
xxvi. 9	Piplei] Pimplei
xxxi. 18	at] et
xxxii. 1	poscimur] poscimus

Odes, Book II

iv. 18   delectam] dilectam
v. 16   petit] petet
x. 9   saepius] saevius
xi. 23   in comptum] incomptum

Odes, Book III

i. 42   sidere] Sidone
iii. 12   bibit] bibet
vii. 20   monet] movet
vii. 24   cave:] cave.
vii. 28   alveo.] alveo,
xxix. 43 vixi;] vixi'
xxix. 48 vexit.'] vexit.

Odes, Book IV

iv. 17   Raeti] Raetis
iv. 10   Ligurinum] Ligurine

SELECT BIBLIOGRAPHY

Bibliographies

Doblhofer, E., *Horaz in der Forschung nach* 1957. Erträge der Forschung, 279 (Darmstadt, 1992).

Harrison, S. J., in *Homage to Horace* below, 349–75.

Kissel, W., 'Horaz 1936–1975: Eine Gesamtbibliographie', in *Aufstieg und Niedergang der Römische Welt*, 2. 31. 3 (Berlin, 1981).

Romano, E., *Q. Orazio Flacco: le opere*, i. *Le* Odi (Rome, 1991).

Translations, Commentaries, Criticism

Carne-Ross, D. S., *Horace in Translation* (London, 1966).

Du Quesnay, I. M. LeM., 'Horace and Maecenas: The Propaganda Value of *Sermones I*', in A. J. Woodman and D. West (eds.), *Poetry and Politics in the Age of Augustus* (Cambridge, 1984), 19–58.

Fraenkel, E., *Horace* (Oxford, 1957).

Harrison, S. J. (ed.), *Homage to Horace: A Bimillenary Celebration*. Varied essays (Oxford, 1995).

Lyne, R. O. A. M., *Horace: Behind the Public Poetry* (New Haven, 1995).

Mankin, D., *Horace* Epodes (Cambridge, 1995).

Martindale, C., and Hopkins, D., *Horace Made New* (Cambridge, 1993).

Michie, J., *The Odes of Horace* (London, 1964). A translation into English verse.

Nisbet, R. G. M., 'Horace's *Epodes* and History', in A. J. Woodman and D. West (eds.), *Poetry and Politics in the Age of Augustus* (Cambridge, 1984), 1–18, reprinted in R. G. M. Nisbet, *Collected Papers on Latin Literature*, ed. S. J. Harrison (Oxford, 1995), 161–81.

—— and Hubbard, M., *Horace* Odes *Book I* (Oxford, 1970).

—— —— *Horace* Odes *Book II* (Oxford, 1978).

Poole, A., and Maule, J., *The Oxford Book of Classical Verse in Translation* (Oxford, 1965).

Sokal, A., 'Transgressing the Boundaries: Toward a Transformative Hermeneutics of Quantum Gravity', *Social Text* (1996).

West, D., *Reading Horace* (Edinburgh, 1967). Mainly on Horace's metaphors.

—— *Horace* Odes I: *Carpe Diem*. Text, translation, and commentary (Oxford, 1995).

Williams, G., *The Third Book of Horace's* Odes (Oxford, 1969).
—— *Horace* (Oxford, 1972). A short introduction.
—— 'Libertino Patre Natus: True or False?', in Harrison, *Homage to Horace*, 296–313.

CHRONOLOGICAL SURVEY

BC	(Early dates traditional)
1090	Fall of Troy
753	Foundation of Rome by Romulus
510	Expulsion of the Tarquins
509	Creation of Roman Republic
264–241	First Punic War
218–201	Second Punic War
218	Hannibal crosses the Alps
202	Scipio Africanus Maior defeats Carthaginians at Zama
149–146	Third Punic War
146	Scipio Africanus Minor destroys Carthage
70	Birth of Virgil
65	Birth of Horace
63	Birth of Octavian
59	First Triumvirate: Caesar, Crassus, and Pompey
53	Crassus defeated by Parthians at Carrhae
44	Caesar assassinated
43	Second Triumvirate: Antony, Lepidus, and Octavian
42	Defeat of Brutus and Cassius at Philippi
39	Virgil, *Eclogues*
38	Virgil introduces Horace to Maecenas
37–36	War against Sextus Pompeius
35	Horace, *Satires* I
33?	Horace receives Sabine farm
31	Octavian defeats Antony and Cleopatra at Actium
30	Death of Antony and Cleopatra in Alexandria
30?	Horace, *Epodes*
29	Virgil, *Georgics*
	Triple triumph of Octavian
28	Temple of Palatine Apollo dedicated
	Propertius, *Elegies* I
27	Octavian takes the name Augustus
26	Tibullus, *Elegies* I
26–5	Augustus campaigns in Spain
23	Horace, *Odes* I–III
	Propertius, *Elegies* II–III
20	Restoration of Crassus' standards and prisoners taken at Carrhae

EPODES

I

Ibis Liburnis

You'll sail, dear friend Maecenas, on your light Liburnians,
    among the galleons tall as fortresses,
ready to take the load of danger Caesar bears
    on your own shoulders.

And what are we to do, since life is sweet for us
    if you survive, and bitter if you die?
Shall we obey you, and pursue a life of ease
    (which gives no pleasure if not shared with you)
or choose this strenuous life and steel ourselves
    to bear what brave men must?   10

We'll bear. Across the ridges of the Alps
    and the inhospitable Caucasus,
or to the furthest bay of all the Western seas
    we'll follow you with fearless heart.

You ask how one as feeble and as frail as I
    could ease your labours by my own?
I will be less afraid if I am at your side.
    Those who are absent suffer most from fear,
just as the mother bird while guarding unfledged chicks
    fears most the serpent's glide   20
when she has left the nest, although her presence
    could not be any help to them.

Gladly I'd fight in this and every other war
    in hopes of pleasing you—
not that more bullocks should be yoked
    to pull my ploughs,
not that before the Dogstar comes my flocks should leave
    Calabria and go to pasture in Lucania,
nor that my gleaming villa high at Tusculum
    should touch the walls of Circe's son.   30

Your kindness has already given me enough
 and more. I shall not gather wealth
to bury in the earth, like stingy Chremes,
 or squander like some feckless fool.

II

Beatus ille

'Fortunate the man who, free from cares,
 like men of old still works
his father's fields with his own oxen,
 encumbered by no debt.
No soldier he, aroused by bugle's blare,
 nor does he fear the angry sea.
The Forum he avoids and lofty doors
 of powerful citizens.

And so, to daughters of the vine when they are come
 of age, he weds tall poplars;   10
in sheltered valley sees his wandering herds
 of lowing cattle;
or with his sickle prunes the useless growth
 and grafts more fruitful shoots;
or stores pressed honey in clean jars;
 or shears his helpless sheep.

When Autumn raises in the fields its head
 with fruit so richly crowned,
with what delight he plucks the pears he grafted
 and grapes that challenge any purple dye, 20
to give to you, Priapus, and Silvanus too,
 the father god, and guardian of his bounds.
He loves to lie beneath an ancient ilex tree,
 or deep in grass too lush to leave,
as all the while the water glides between high banks,
 and birds are moaning in the woods,
and leaves speak out against the flowing stream,
 and every sound invites to easy sleep.

But when the thunder of Jove's winter season
    musters the rains and snows,   30
with all his dogs on every side he drives
    wild boar into his ring of nets,
or stretches wide-meshed toils on twigs he's smoothed
    to trap the greedy thrushes,
and hunts the timid hare and crane migrating
    to his snare—delicious prey.
Amid these pleasures who would not forget
    the miseries brought on by love?

But if chaste wife were there to play her part
    and make the home and children sweet,   40
like Sabine women, or like sun-scorched wife
    of busy farmer in Apulia,
she'd heap the sacred hearth with seasoned logs
    to wait her weary husband's coming,
shutting the lusty flock in wattle pens
    and milking swollen udders,
decanting this year's wine from its sweet cask,
    and setting out a meal unbought.

Then oysters from the Lucrine Lake would hold no charm
    for me, nor turbot, nor the parrot-wrasse,   50
if storms of thunder rumbling in the East should drive
    them into our Italian sea.
No guinea fowl from Africa nor heathcock from Ionia
    would then go down my throat
so tastily as the choice olives picked
    from richest branches of my trees,
or sorrel leaf that loves our meadowlands,
    or mallows so digestible for invalids,
or lamb killed on the holy day of Terminus,
    or kid snatched from the wolf.   60
At such a feast what pleasure it would give to see
    the full-fed sheep all hurry home,
to see the weary oxen drag on sluggish necks
    their plough with share upturned,
while houseborn slaves, the rich hive's swarm,
    stand by the hearth around its smiling gods.'

When Alfius, the money lender said all this,
    resolved at last, at last, to be a countryman,
he called in all his money on the Ides—
    and on the Kalends now he tries to place it out again.   70

III

Parentis olim

If any man with impious hand has broken
    his aged father's neck,
let him eat garlic. It is worse than hemlock.
    Peasants must have guts of brass.
What is this poison seething in my chest?
    I am betrayed. These herbs
were cooked in viper's blood or else Canidia
    has touched this filthy food.

When among all the comely Argonauts, Medea saw
    and marvelled at their leader Jason,   10
before he went to yoke the still unbroken bulls,
    she smeared the garlic on him,
and then before she fled on serpent wings, in garlic steeped
    her gifts to take revenge on his new whore.
The stars have never sent such heat to brood
    on parched Apulia.
It was no fiercer fire that scorched the back
    of mighty Hercules.

And if you ever take in mind to try a trick like this,
    my sly Maecenas, I do pray   20
your lover may put up her hand against your kiss
    and lie far from you on the bed.

IV

Lupis et agnis

Fate has decreed that wolves and lambs should be
    no more at odds than you and me.

Your flanks are scorched by Spanish ropes,
  your legs by iron chains,
and though you strut about in pride of wealth,
  good fortune does not mend low blood.
Do you not see as you pace out the Sacred Way
  with toga three yards wide,
how passers-by all turn their heads
  in undisguised disgust?   10
'Cut as he was by the triumvirs' lash
  until the crier wearied of it,
he farms a thousand good Falernian acres now
  and with his coach wears out the Appian Way.
There at the front the great knight sits
  and makes a mockery of Otho's law.
Why send so many ships
  with two-ton beaks
against the pirates and the bands of slaves
  if this, yes this, is what we call our admiral?'   20

V

At, o deorum

'By all the gods in heaven who rule
  the earth and race of men,
what is this uproar? Why are all your faces
  so turned on me, and all so cruel?
I beg you by your children, if you ever called
  in honest childbirth on Lucina and she came,
and by the empty honour of the purple that I wore,
  by Jupiter's revulsion from this act—
why gaze at me as though you were my stepmother,
  or some wild beast at bay?'   10

With quavering voice the boy appealed,
  stripped of his finery,
naked, enough to soften the most godless heart
  in all of Thrace,
but there Canidia, with tiny vipers binding
  her tangled hair,

commanded them to dig out fig trees from the graves,
  to bring her funeral cypresses,
to gather eggs and feathers of the screech-owl, bird of night,
  and soak them in the blood of loathsome toads,   20
to pick whatever herbs Iolcus grows
  and poison-rich Hiberia,
and rip the bones from starving bitches' jaws—
  and burn all this on Colchian fires.

But Sagana was rushing through the house,
  sprinkling the waters of Avernus as she went.
She looked like some sea urchin, with her bristling hair,
  or like a wild boar on the charge.

And Veia, conscienceless, scooped out the earth
  with iron-bladed mattock.   30
Groaning she worked to bury him,
  where each long day the boy
would three times see the rich fare served to him,
  and seeing it, would die,
only his face above the ground,
  like swimmers treading water—
all to cut out his liver and the marrow of his bones
  and dry them as an aphrodisiac,
when once the pupils of his eyes, long fixed on food
  forbidden him, were wasted into nothing.   40

And Folia was there from Ariminum—
  her lusts were those of men—
so went the idle gossip in Neapolis
  and all the neighbouring towns.
She can bewitch the moon and stars with her Thessalian
    chants
  and pluck them from the sky.

Savage Canidia now, with blackened teeth
  gnawing her long-nailed thumb,
what did she say? What did she fail to say?
  'O faithful witnesses of this my life,   50
dark Night, and you, Diana, queen of silence when
  the secret rituals are performed,

be present now, turn now your wrath and holy power
  against the houses of my enemies.
While deep in fearful woods the savage beasts
  lie resting in their grateful sleep,
may all Subura's bitches bark and all men mock
  the old adulterer,
steeped in my spikenard—a picture
  perfect and far beyond my art to paint.   60
But what is this? Why do Medea's eastern drugs,
  so deadly once, now fail?
With these she took revenge upon her husband's bride,
  proud daughter of great Creon,
who wore her gift, imbued with putrid gore,
  and died in fire before Medea's flight.
And yet no herb, no root, in rough and secret places
    growing,
  escaped my search,
and any bed that Varus slept in was besmeared to bring
  forgetfulness of all his other loves.   70
Alas! alas! he walks the streets, freed by the spell
  of some enchantress still more expert than myself.
O Varus, Varus, you will have good cause to weep.
  No ordinary potions now will drag
you running back to me. Your senses will return,
  reclaimed by spells the Marsians never knew.
I shall prepare a stronger brew and pour a stronger
    draught
  to tempt your dainty taste,
and sky shall sooner sink below the sea, and sooner earth
  shall lie spread out above them both,   80
than you will cease to blaze with love for me,
  as this pitch blazes with black flames.'

At this the boy no longer sought to soothe
  the godless hags,
nor did he know how best to break his silence,
  but uttered these Thyestean prayers:
'Your magic poisons may change wrong to right and right to
    wrong,

but cannot alter men's deserts.
With curses I shall harry you. No sacrifice will expiate
    my bitter hatred,   90
and when at your command I breathe my last,
    I'll haunt you as a Fury in the night,
my ghost will slash your faces with its claws
    —this is within the powers of the gods below—
and, perching on your restless hearts,
    instead of sleep I'll give you fear.
With stones the rabble from all sides will batter you
    from street to street, you filthy crones,
and wolves and carrion vultures of the Esquiline
    will mangle your unburied limbs.   100
When I am dead, my parents, O alas!
    will live to see that sight.

VI

Quid immerentis hospites

Why pester harmless passers-by, you cringing cur?
    Are you afraid of wolves?
Why not direct your empty threats my way and yap
    at one who'll bite you back?
Like tawny Spartan or Molossian hound,
    the shepherd's dangerous friends,
I'll prick my ears up and will chase through deepest snow
    whatever beast will run from me.
But all you do is fill the woods with fearful noise,
    then come and sniff the scraps men throw for you.   10
Beware! Beware! I make short work of rogues.
    My horns are ready and they're up.
Remember false Lycambes and the son-in-law he spurned,
    think of the rough-tongued enemy of Bupalo,
and don't imagine if you come at me with poison tooth,
    I'll burst out weeping like a helpless boy.

VII

Quo, quo, scelesti ruitis?

Why this mad rush to join a wicked war? Your swords
    were sheathed. Why do you draw them now?
Perhaps too little Latin blood has poured upon the plains
    and into Neptune's sea,
not so that Rome could burn the lofty citadels
    of Carthage, her great enemy,
or that the Briton, still beyond our reach, should walk
    the Sacred Way in chains,
but so that Rome might fall by Roman hands
    and answer all the prayers of Parthia.   10
This never was the way of lions or of wolves
    to shed the blood of their own kind.
Is it blind madness, or some deadlier force?
    Some ancient guilt? Give answer now.

Silence, and pallor on the face,
    minds numbed with shock.

The case is made. It is harsh Fate that drives
    the Romans, and the crime of fratricide
since Remus' blameless lifeblood poured upon the ground—
    a curse to generations yet unborn.   20

VIII

Rogare longo

You dare to ask me, you decrepit, stinking slut,
    what makes me impotent?
And you with blackened teeth, and so advanced
    in age that wrinkles plough your forehead,
your raw and filthy arsehole gaping like a cow's
    between your wizened buttocks.
It's your slack breasts that rouse me (I have seen
    much better udders on a mare)

your flabby paunch and scrawny thighs
    stuck on your swollen ankles.   10

May you be blessed with wealth! May effigies
    of triumphators march you to the grave,
and may no other wife go on parade
    weighed down with fatter pearls!

But why do Stoic tracts so love to lie
    on your silk cushions?
They won't cause big erections or delay the droop—
    you know that penises can't read.
If that is what you want from my fastidious groin,
    your mouth has got some work to do.   20

IX

Quando repostum

When shall I celebrate great Caesar's victory and drink
    the Caecuban laid down for sacred feasts
with you, heaven-blest Maecenas, in the lofty home
    the gods have given you,
to mingled music of the lyre and pipe,
    Dorian the one, the other barbarous?
Just so not long ago we drank when Neptune's admiral
    was routed and his galleys fired,
although he once had threatened Rome with chains
    struck off his friends, our treacherous slaves.   10

Now Romans are a woman's slaves—O hear you this
    you generations yet to come—
carrying arms and stakes for her, and at the beck and call
    of wrinkled eunuchs,
and there the sun among our eagles sees
    —the shame of it—mosquito nets!

But now two thousand Galli, hailing Caesar, have wheeled
    their snorting mounts to join with us,
and the opposing ships have pulled to port

and lie there cowering in the Ambracian Gulf. 20
Io Triumphe! Bring your chariots of gold
    and oxen never yoked.
Io Triumphe! From Jugurtha's war you did not bring
    a greater warrior home to Rome,
Not even Africanus equalled him, whose valour made
    a sepulchre where Carthage once had stood.

Conquered by land and sea, the foe soon changed
    his purple cloak for mourning black.
Either he flies to glorious hundred-citied Crete
    carried by winds he did not choose, 30
or steers towards the Syrtes where the southerlies hold sway,
    or sails the sea he knows not where.

Bring more capacious goblets, boy,
    and Chian wine and Lesbian,
or dose us with the Caecuban
    —seasickness must be checked.
What joy to end anxiety and fear
    for Caesar's fate with sweet Lyaeus!

X

Mala soluta navis

Under an evil star the ship set out to sea
    that bore the stinking Maevius.

Fail not, O Auster blowing from the south, to pound it port
    and starboard with great waves,
let Eurus from the east upturn the sea,
    scattering the broken oars and ropes,
and from the north let huge Aquilo rise, the wind that breaks
    the ilex trembling on the mountain tops.
Let not a friendly star be seen that night
    as fierce Orion sets, 10
but let it be a sea as wild as that which bore
    victorious Greeks from Troy

when Pallas from Troy's ashes turned her wrath
    upon the godless ship of Ajax.

The crew will sweat, how they will sweat,
    and your own face go green,
and there will be such womanly wailing then
    and prayers to an unhearing Jupiter
while shrieks the Ionic Gulf and streaming Notus
    shatters the keel.   20

If then rich pickings lie upon the curving shore
    and feed the gulls,
the gods of tempest will receive a sacrifice—
    a randy billy-goat and lamb.

XI

Petti, nihil me

    It gives no joy to me as once it did
Pettius, to write little verses in the throes of love,
    love that demands that I should dote
more than anyone else upon pretty boys and girls.

    The third December now has stripped the glory
from the trees since my passion for Inachia ended.
    Through all the city—and I am ashamed of it—
I was a laughing stock. I can't face my friends.
    My apathy, my silence,
my deep-drawn sighs, told them I was in love.   10

    'Is money all she wants? And are
a poor man's qualities no good to her?' I'd weep and wail
    to you the moment that the shameless god
warmed me with the heat of wine and dragged out my secrets.

    'But now if I would let the bile boil in my breast,
I'd soon scatter to the winds these hateful remedies
    that never yet have cured my illness,
I'd lose all shame and give up the uneven battle.'

    This was the sturdy course I chose when in your company.
You'd then tell me to go home and I'd drift to her doorposts—

Heavens! how unkind they were to me—and threshold—
Heavens! it was hard—it broke my hips and ribs.   22

   But now Lyciscus is my love
and he boasts he's prettier than any mere woman could be.
   From him no freely given advice
of friends nor rough abuse can separate me.
   Another passion might, for some lovely girl,
or a slender boy with his long hair tied up behind in a knot.

XII

Quid tibi vis

'What are you after? It's black elephants you should mate with!
   Why send me presents? Why write me letters?
I'm no sturdy youngster. I don't have a big fat nose.
   But I can sniff the polyp in *your* nose
or stinking billy in your hairy armpits quicker
   than keenest hound can scent the wild boar's lair.'

The sweat and nasty smell get worse all over
   her wrinkled body, as my penis droops
and raging passion cools
   and all the while the powdered chalk   10
and crocodile-shit dye run on her face as she ruts away,
   breaking the bed and the canopy over it,
and giving me an earful for being so choosy:

   'You're not so slack when lying with Inachia.
Inachia you manage three times a night, but you flop
   at the thought of doing me once. To hell with Lesbia
who gave me a wimp when I looked for a bull, and all the time
   Amyntas of Cos was mine for the taking,
with a tool in his great groin sturdier than
   a deeply rooted sapling in the mountains.   20
You ask what's all the hurry. Who are these woollens for,
   all double steeped in Tyrian dyes? For you, of course,
so that when you're with your friends, there will be nobody
   whose trollop loves him more than I love you.

O! I'm so sad. You've run from me like the lamb in panic
  from the wicked wolf, or roe-deer from the lion.'

XIII

Horrida tempestas

This fearsome storm has shrunk the sky, and rain
  and snow bring Jupiter himself down on our heads.
Seas roar, trees howl in northerlies from Thrace; let's seize
  the moment, friends, and while our knees are spry and
    while
with decency we may, let's smooth away the frown of age.
  You there, bring wine pressed in the year of my
    Torquatus.
Forget the rest; God will perhaps put all to rights again,
  a gentler time will come. Now soak your heads
in Persian spikenard, and with Cyllenian lyre lighten
  the heart of grim anxieties,   10
as the great Centaur to his mighty pupil sang and prophesied:

'Invincible in war, the goddess Thetis' mortal son, for you
there waits the land of old Assaracus, through which there
    flows
  Scamander's icy trickle and Simois' gliding stream.
The Fates, who do not err, have cut your thread.
  Your mother will not bring you home on her blue waters.
While there, be sure to lighten all your ills with wine and
    song,
  sweet comforts for the ugliness of pain.'

XIV

Mollis inertia

Why am I so effete? Why has this idleness
  in deep oblivion drowned my every sense

as though my thirsty throat had drained great cups
    of Lethe's sleep? You wear me out,
Maecenas, candid friend, so often asking this.

    It is the god, the god, I say,
forbids me reach the roller of these epodes
    I promised long ago.

Just so Anacreon of Teos burned
    for Samian Bathyllus   10
and often on the lyre bewailed his love
    in artless song.
So you yourself are fired by passion. Since no lovelier flame
    than yours consumed the towers of Troy,
then glory in your fate, while Phryne, once a slave,
    makes me (and many others) simmer.

XV

Nox erat et caelo

'Twas night and in the cloudless sky the moon
    shone out among the lesser stars,
when you first took your solemn oath to me,
    mocking the majesty of the almighty gods.
You swore our mutual love would never die,
    that you would cling tighter than ivy winds
its coils around the towering mountain oak,
    while wolves are enemies to sheep, Orion churns
the winter sea for those who sail on it,
    and breezes blow Apollo's unshorn hair.   10

But you, Neaera, as I am a man, will suffer for it.
    For if there is in Flaccus any virtue,
he will not see you give his rival all your nights.
    He's angry now, he'll look for some true love,
and his resolve when he is roused is proof against your beauty,
    once bitterness has settled in his heart.

But you, who are more fortunate, and strut around
    jeering at my distress,

though you were rich with flocks and herds, and Pactolus
    rolled down its floods of gold for you,   20
although Pythagoras reborn had taught you all his secret lore,
    and you were fairer far than Nireus,
when she moves on, your turn will come to weep,
    and mine to laugh.

XVI

Altera iam teritur

A second generation is ground down by civil wars,
    and Rome is falling, ruined by the might of Rome.
What Marsian neighbours never could destroy,
    nor hostile armies of Etruscan Porsena,
nor Capua's ambitious courage, nor the bravery
    of Spartacus, nor false, rebellious Allobrox,
nor savage blue-eyed warriors of Germany,
    nor Hannibal, so hated by our ancestors,
this city we, this doomed and godless generation, shall destroy,
    wild beasts will soon take back the land,   10
barbarian conquerors will stand upon the smouldering ash,
    their cavalry will pound the earth with sounding hooves,
and, jeering, scatter to the winds and suns—the sin is ours—
    the hallowed bones of Romulus.

Perhaps you all are asking, or the best of you,
    how we can free ourselves from this harsh fate?

One course alone there is—just as
    Phocaeans swore an oath and left
their fields and gods and shrines to be the homes
    of ravening wolves and boars,   20
so let us go where our feet take us, where
    south wind and fierce southwester call across the waves.
Agreed? Is any better course proposed?
    Then let's aboard while omens still allow.

But let us swear that we shall not return till rocks
    rise from the bottom of the sea and float,

we shall not turn our sails for home until the River Po
    washes the summits of the Matine hills,
and soaring Apennines rush down into the sea;
    till monstrous couplings join wild beasts in lusts   30
unheard-of, until tigress ruts with stag
    and doves commit adultery with hawks;
till trusting cattle cease to fear the tawny lion's roar,
    and goats grow scales and swim the salty seas.

These oaths now let us swear, and any others that cut off
    fond hopes of our return. Let us all go, or those at least
above the ignorant and common herd. The weak and hopeless
    let them stay and burden their doomed beds.
But you, who have some manhood in you, do not wail
    like women, rather fly along the Etruscan coast.   40
The Ocean wandering round the earth awaits us now.
    So let us seek the Blessed Fields and Wealthy Isles,
where every year the land unploughed gives grain,
    and vines unpruned are never out of flower,
and olive shoots unfailing bud, and set their fruit,
    and dusky fig ungrafted graces its own tree,
the honey flows from hollow ilex, and from hills
    the streamlet lightly leaps with sounding footfall.
There to the milking pails unbidden come the goats,
    and friendly flocks their swollen udders bring.   50
When evening comes no howling bear patrols the pens,
    no viper heaves its mound of earth.

Enchanted, we shall wonder at it all—how rainy easterlies
    do never scour the fields with storms of rain,
and how our juicy seeds are never scorched in dried-up
        earth—
    the king of heaven tempers both extremes.
Here Argo's oarsman never drove the pine,
    nor unchaste Colchian ever set her foot,
and to this land Sidonian sailors never turned their yards
    nor toiled Ulysses' crew.   60
No plague infects the flocks, no star
    scorches the herds with raging heat.

These shores were set apart by Jupiter for righteous men
    when he debased the Golden Age
with bronze, then hardened it with iron. From these ills
    the righteous can escape, and I shall be their prophet.

XVII

Iam iam efficaci

'I yield, I yield, to your most potent science,
and beg you by the kingdom of Proserpina,
and by unpitying Diana's powers,
and by the books of mighty incantations
which can unfix the stars and call them down to earth,
leave off, Canidia, at last your sacred spells,
loosen, o loosen your swift wheel, and drive it back.

Once Telephus was pitied by the Nereid's son,
although against him he had led the Mysians,
and hurled at him his sharp-tipped spear.   10
And once man-slaying Hector was assigned as prey
to carrion birds and dogs, but when the king, heartbroken,
had left his city walls and thrown himself at cruel Achilles' feet,
the Trojan mothers were allowed at last to mourn.
Once too, Ulixes, much-enduring, saw his crew
put off their bristles and their hides
with Circe's blessing, mind and voice
restored and their old dignity of countenance.

Darling of salesmen and of sailing men,
have you not punished me enough, and more?   20
My youth, my blushing pink has gone, and left
me yellow skin and bone, my hair is white
thanks to your unguents, and my pain has no relief,
night follows close on day and day on night,
and never any respite for my panting breast.

And so I am defeated and believe what I denied—
Sabellan incantations sound all through my heart.

My head is bursting with your Marsian spells.
What more do you desire? O land and sea, I burn
as Hercules once burned when smeared   30
with the black blood of Nessus. Hotter far
I burn than Etna's flowering flame in Sicily.
You are a crucible of Colchian drugs
reducing me to ashes to be blown in vicious winds.
What end is there for me? What payment can I make?
Tell me and I shall pay the penalty in full,
eager to make atonement, with a hundred bulls
if so you wish, or if you ask, to sound
on a deceitful lyre: "O chaste and virtuous lady,
you'll walk among the stars, a constellation all of gold."   40

Although indignant at the slur on Helen, Castor
and Castor's mighty brother, overcome by prayers,
restored the eyes to the great poet they had blinded.
And so I now ask you—and you have power to grant—
relieve my madness. You are stained by no ancestral shame,
you are no harridan to haunt the paupers' graves,
a ninth-day expert rummaging among the ash,
your heart hospitable, your hands so pure,
and Pactumeius is your son. Yours was the blood
that stained the clothes the midwife washed, although   50
you always looked so lively, leaping from your bed of pain.'

'Why pour out prayers? My ears are blocked,
deafer than winter rocks to cries of naked sailors
when Neptune's towering breakers pound the shore.
You make a laughing stock of our Cotytian rites,
the sacraments of unrestricted lust,
you Sorcerer Supreme, High Pontiff of the Esquiline,
you blab my name round Rome and hope to live?
Much good it did me to enrich Paelignian hags,
and brew more speedy poisons. Now for you   60
death will not come as quickly as your prayers implore.
The only reason to drag out your wretched life
is to endure an endless prospect of fresh miseries.

Dishonest Pelops' father, Tantalus, prays for repose,
abundant food before his eyes, but always out of reach.

Prometheus, chained to receive the vulture's visit, prays.
The prayer of Sisyphus is to be allowed to push
his rock up to the mountain top. Jove's laws forbid.
You soon in weariness and anguish and despair,
will wish to leap from some high tower,   70
to take a Noric sword and open up your breast,
to tie a noose around your neck—to no avail.
Then shall I be the rider on your loathsome back
and all the world shall bow before my arrogance.

Or do you think that I, who can cause waxen images
to move, as you have found by prying, and pluck
the moon from heaven by my spells,
who can arouse cremated corpses,
and blend the elixirs of lust—do you believe that I
shall weep because my arts are powerless against you?'   80

ODES

ODES, BOOK I

I

Maecenas atavis edite

Maecenas, sprung from an ancient line of kings,
my stronghold, my pride, and my delight,
some like to collect Olympic dust
on their chariots, and if their scorching wheels

graze the turning-post and they win the palm of glory,
they become lords of the earth and rise to the gods;
one man is pleased if the fickle mob of Roman citizens
competes to lift him up to triple honours;

another, if he stores away in his own granary
the sweepings from all the threshing-floors of Libya;   10
the man who enjoys cleaving his ancestral fields
with the mattock, you could never move, not with the legacy

of Attalus, to become a frightened sailor
cutting the Myrtoan sea with Cyprian timbers;
the merchant, terrified at the brawl of African gale
with Icarian waves, is all for leisure and the countryside

round his own home town, but he is soon rebuilding
his shattered ships—he cannot learn to endure poverty;
there is a man who sees no objection to drinking
old Massic wine or taking time out of the day,   20

stretched out sometimes under the green arbutus,
sometimes by a gently welling spring of sacred water;
many enjoy the camp, the sound of the trumpet merged
in the bugle, the wars that mothers

abhor; the huntsman stays out under a cold sky,
and forgets his tender wife the moment
his faithful dogs catch sight of a hind
or a Marsian boar bursts his delicate nets.

As for me, it is ivy, the reward of learned brows,
that puts me among the gods above. As for me,   30
the cold grove and the light-footed choruses of Nymphs
and Satyrs set me apart from the people

if Euterpe lets me play her pipes, and Polyhymnia
does not withhold the lyre of Lesbos.
But if you enrol me among the lyric bards
my soaring head will touch the stars.

II

Iam satis terris

Father Jupiter has already sent enough fierce hail
and snow, and his red right arm
has struck his holy citadel bringing
    fear to the city

and fear to the nations. The cruel age of Pyrrha seemed
to be returning and the strange sights she had to bewail—
Proteus driving his herds to visit
    the high mountains,

shoals of fishes sticking in the tops of elms
where once the doves had nested,   10
and frightened deer swimming in seas hurled down
    upon the earth.

We have seen yellow Tiber wrench back his waves
from the Tuscan shore and rush
to throw down king Numa's memorials
    and Vesta's temple,

eager to avenge the shrill grievances
of Ilia his wife. Without the blessing of Jupiter
this doting husband left his course and flooded
    his left bank.   20

Young men will hear that citizen sharpened against citizen
swords that should have slain our Persian enemies. They will
    hear—

what few there are, thanks to the sins of their fathers—
  of the battles we fought.

What god can the people call upon to shore up
their crumbling empire? What prayer can the Virgins
din into the ears of Vesta who does not listen
  to their chanting?

To whom will Jupiter give the task of expiating
our crime? Come at long last, we pray,   30
your white shoulders veiled in cloud,
  augur Apollo;

or you come if you prefer, smiling Venus of Eryx,
with Jest and Cupid hovering round you;
or, if you take thought for the race you founded
  and your neglected descendants,

come, god of war, sated with your long sport,
exulting in the battle cry, in polished helmets,
in the face of the Marsian foot soldier showing no pity
  for his bleeding enemy;   40

or if you, Mercury, winged son of bountiful Maia,
have changed shape and are imitating
a young man on the earth, accepting the name
  of Caesar's avenger,

do not return too soon to the sky. For long years
be pleased to stay with the people of Romulus,
and may no breeze come and snatch you up too soon,
  angered by our sins.

Here rather celebrate your triumphs.
Here delight to be hailed as Father and Princeps   50
and do not allow the Medes to ride unavenged
  while you, Caesar, are our leader.

III

Sic te diva

O ship, to whom Virgil has been entrusted
and who has to repay that debt, may the goddess

who rules over Cyprus, may Helen's brothers,
those shining stars, and the father of the winds,

shutting them all up except the nor'wester Iapyx,
govern your sailing, if only you deliver Virgil safe,
I pray you, to the boundaries of Attica,
and preserve half of my soul.

Oak and triple bronze
were round the breast of the man who first committed   10
a fragile ship to the truculent sea.
He was not afraid of the swooping sou'wester

battling it out with the winds of the north,
nor the weeping Hyades, nor the madness of the south wind,
the supreme judge of when to raise
and when to lay the Adriatic sea.

He did not fear the approaching step of death,
but looked with dry eyes on monsters swimming,
on ocean boiling, and on
the ill-famed Acroceraunian rocks.   20

In vain in his wise foresight did God sever
the lands of the earth by means of the dividing sea,
if impious ships yet leap
across waters which they should not touch.

Boldly enduring everything,
the human race rushes to forbidden sin.
Boldly the offspring of Iapetus brought down fire
by wicked deceit to the peoples of the earth.

After the theft of fire from its home
in the heavens, wasting disease and a cohort   30
of new fevers fell upon the earth
and the slow necessity of death, once so remote,

speeded its step.
Daedalus ventured upon the empty air
with wings not meant for man.
The labour of Hercules burst through Acheron.

For mortals no height is too steep:
in our stupidity we try to scale the very heavens
    and by our wickedness we do not allow
Jupiter to lay down his angry thunderbolts.   40

IV

Solvitur acris hiems

Harsh winter is melting away in the welcome change to spring
    and zephyrs,
    winches are pulling down dry-bottomed ships,
the cattle no longer like the steading, the ploughman does not
    hug the fire,
    and meadows are not white with hoar-frost.

Venus of Cythera leads on the dance beneath a hanging
    moon,
    and the lovely Graces, linking arms with Nymphs,
shake the ground with alternate feet, while burning Vulcan
    visits the grim foundries of the Cyclopes.

Now is the time to oil the hair and bind the head with green
    myrtle
    or flowers born of the earth now freed from frost;   10
now too is the time to sacrifice to Faunus in shady groves
    whether he asks a lamb or prefers a kid.

Pale death kicks with impartial foot at the hovels of the poor
    and the towers of kings. O fortunate Sestius,
the brief sum of life does not allow us to start on long
    hopes.
    You will soon be kept close by Night and the fabled
    shades

in Pluto's meagre house. When you go there
    you will no longer cast lots to rule the wine,
nor admire tender Lycidas, whom all the young men
    now burn for and for whom the girls will soon be
    warm.   20

V

Quis multa gracilis

What slim youngster soaked in perfumes
is hugging you now, Pyrrha, on a bed of roses
    deep in your lovely cave? For whom
        are you tying up your blonde hair?

You're so elegant and so simple. Many's the time
he'll weep at your faithlessness and the changing gods,
    and be amazed at seas
        roughened by black winds,

but now in all innocence he enjoys your golden beauty
and imagines you always available, always lovable,   10
    not knowing about treacherous breezes—
        I pity poor devils who have no experience of you

and are dazzled by your radiance. As for me,
the tablet on the temple wall announces
    that I have dedicated my dripping clothes
        to the god who rules the sea.

VI

Scriberis Vario

Varius, the eagle of Homeric song, will write
of your valour and your victories, all the feats
of formidable soldiers fighting under your command
    on ship or on horseback.

We do not attempt, Agrippa, to speak of these things,
nor of the bad temper of Peleus' son who did not know
how to yield, nor of the voyages of Ulixes the double-dealer,
    nor of the savage house of Pelops.

We are too slight for these large themes. Modesty
and the Muse who commands the unwarlike lyre forbid us
to diminish the praise of glorious Caesar and yourself   11
    by our imperfect talent.

Who could write worthily of Mars girt in adamantine tunic,
or Meriones, black with the dust of Troy,
or the son of Tydeus, who with the help of Pallas Athene
was the equal of the gods?

What we sing of is drinking parties, of battles fought
by fierce virgins with nails cut sharp to wound young men.
Sometimes we are fancy free, sometimes a little moved,
cheerfully, after our fashion.   20

VII

Laudabunt alii

Others will praise bright Rhodes or Mytilene or Ephesus
or the walls of Corinth with its two seas,
Thebes famous for Bacchus or Delphi for Apollo
or Thessalian Tempe;

there are those whose one task is to celebrate the city
of chaste Pallas in unbroken song,
and to sport on their brows a crown of olive plucked
wherever
they find it; in honour of Juno many a one

will speak of wealthy Mycenae and horse-rearing Argos.
As for me, I am not so struck   10
by much-enduring Lacedaemon or the fat plain of Larisa,
as by Albunea's sounding home

and the plunging Anio, by the grove of Tiburnus and its
orchards
watered by swiftly flowing streams.
The bright south wind will often wipe the clouds from the
dark sky.
It is not always pregnant with rain.

So you too, Plancus, would be wise to remember to put a stop
to sadness and the labours of life
with mellow, undiluted wine, whether you are in camp among
the gleaming standards or whether you will be   20

in the deep shade of your beloved Tibur. When Teucer was
    on the run
    from Salamis and his father, they say that nevertheless,
awash with wine, he bound his brow with a crown of poplar
    leaves
    and spoke these words to his grieving friends:

'Allies and comrades, Fortune is kinder than a father.
    Wherever she takes us, there shall we go. Do not despair
while Teucer takes the auspices and Teucer is your leader.
    Apollo does not err and he has promised

that in a new land we shall find a second Salamis.
    You are brave men and have often suffered worse   30
with me. Drive away your cares with wine. Tomorrow
    we shall set out again upon the broad sea.'

VIII

Lydia, dic, per omnis

Tell me, Lydia, by all the gods I beg you,
why you are in such a hurry to destroy Sybaris with your love.
    And why is he deserting the sunny Campus?
He never used to complain about dust or heat.

    Why is he not on horseback and training
for war with his young friends? Why is he not disciplining
    Gallic mouths with jagged bits?
Why is he afraid to put his toe in the yellow Tiber?

    Why does he avoid athletes' oil
like vipers' blood and why are his arms no longer bruised   10
    with weapons, this champion of the discus,
champion of the javelin, so often throwing beyond the mark?

    Why does he hide as the son of Thetis
the sea-goddess hid, so they say, before the tears and deaths
    of Troy, in case his man's clothes
should send him off to the killing and the Lycian cohorts?

IX

Vides ut alta

You see Soracte standing white and deep
with snow, the woods in trouble, hardly able
    to carry their burden, and the rivers
      halted by sharp ice.

Thaw out the cold. Pile up the logs
on the hearth and be more generous, Thaliarchus,
    as you draw the four-year-old Sabine
      from its two-eared cask.

Leave everything else to the gods. As soon as
they still the winds battling it out   10
    on the boiling sea, the cypresses stop waving
      and the old ash trees.

Don't ask what will happen tomorrow.
Whatever day Fortune gives you, enter it
    as profit, and don't look down on love
      and dancing while you're still a lad,

while the gloomy grey keeps away from the green.
Now is the time for the Campus and the squares
    and soft sighs at the time arranged
      as darkness falls.   20

Now is the time for the lovely laugh from the secret corner
giving away the girl in her hiding-place,
    and for the token snatched from her arm
      or finger feebly resisting.

X

Mercuri, facunde

Mercury, eloquent grandson of Atlas,
who cunningly moulded the brutish ways of early man
with the gift of speech and the beauty
    of the wrestling school,

of you shall I sing, messenger of mighty Jupiter
and the gods, father of the curved lyre,
ingenious concealer of whatever in your mischief
    you decide to steal.

Once when you were a baby and Apollo was booming
terrifying threats if you did not return the cattle   10
you had stolen, he suddenly missed his quiver
    and burst out laughing.

Then you escorted Priam when he left Troy
laden with riches, and the haughty sons of Atreus,
the Thessalian watch-fires, and the camp of Troy's enemies
    were all deceived.

You guide the souls of the righteous
to their blessed seats, and with golden staff you herd
the unsubstantial shades, dear to the gods above
    and to the gods below.   20

XI

Tu ne quaesieris

Don't you ask, Leuconoe—the gods do not wish it to be
    known—
what end they have given to me or to you, and don't meddle
    with
Babylonian horoscopes. How much better to accept whatever
    comes,
whether Jupiter gives us other winters or whether this is our
    last

now wearying out the Tyrrhenian sea on the pumice stones
opposing it. Be wise, strain the wine and cut back long
    hope
into a small space. Even as we speak, envious time
flies past. Harvest the day and leave as little as possible
    for tomorrow.

XII

Quem virum aut heroa

What man or hero do you choose, Clio,
to celebrate with lyre or shrill pipe?
What god? Whose name will the playful echo
    sing back

on the shady slopes of Helicon
or on Pindus or chilly Haemus,
from where the wilful woods followed
    sweet-voiced Orpheus,

as by his mother's art he held back swift winds
and the rushing flow of rivers,   10
and led the long-eared oaks with the charm
    of his singing lyre?

What can I do but follow custom and praise first
the Father who governs from hour to hour
the affairs of men and gods,
    the land, and sea, and sky?

None of his children is greater than himself.
There is no living thing like him
or second to him, but at his side Pallas has taken
    the place of honour.   20

Nor shall I be silent about you, Bacchus,
bold in battle, nor the virgin goddess,
enemy of wild beasts, nor you, dread Phoebus
    with your unerring arrow.

I shall speak too of Hercules and of the sons
of Leda, famous for their victories, one with horses
the other with fists. As soon as sailors see
    their bright star shining,

the heaving seas stream down from the rocks,
winds fall, and clouds disperse   30
and when they will it, the towering wave
    subsides upon the ocean.

After these I am at a loss whether to speak of Romulus,
or the peaceful reign of Pompilius,
or the proud rods of Tarquin,
   or Cato's noble death.

With the glorious Muse of Italy I shall gratefully sing
of Regulus and the Scauri, of Paulus prodigal
of his mighty spirit in the victory over Carthage,
   and of Fabricius.   40

Sound in battle, like rough-bearded Curius
and like Camillus he was born
of cruel poverty on his father's farm
   with household gods to match.

The fame of Marcellus grows like a tree,
unseen over time; the Julian Star shines
among them all like the moon
   among the lesser fires.

O father and guardian of the human race,
offspring of Saturn, to whom the Fates have given   50
care over great Caesar, may you reign
   with Caesar second to you.

Whether he routs the Parthians who threaten Latium,
or the Chinese and Indians lying close
to the shore of the sunrise, subduing them
   in a just triumph,

as your subordinate he will rule a joyful world in equity;
you will shake Olympus with the weight of your chariot,
you will send down your angry lightning
   on the groves of the impure.   60

XIII

Cum tu, Lydia

When you praise Telephus's
rosy neck, Lydia, and Telephus's

waxen arms, Oh how my liver
boils and swells in indigestible bile.

At such a time neither mind nor colour
stays in its fixed seat, and moisture trickles furtively
   on to my cheeks making clear how slow
    are the fires macerating me through and through.

I burn if drunken brawling
sullies your white shoulders,   10
   or if that young ruffian's teeth
    print their tell-tale mark upon your lips.

If only you would listen to me,
you would not imagine that he would be for ever
   barbarously bruising those sweet lips
    dipped by Venus in the quintessence of her nectar.

Three times blessed and more than three
and those held in an unbroken bond, whose love
   untorn by scolding or bad temper
will not release them till their last day comes.   20

XIV

O navis, referent

O ship! Will new waves carry you out to sea
again? What are you doing? Make boldly
   for the harbour. Don't you see how
    your side is stripped of its oars,

your mast is crippled by the swift sou'wester,
the yards are groaning, and without roping
   the hull has little chance of holding out
    against the mounting tyranny

of the sea? Your sails are unsound and so are the gods
you call upon once again in dire distress.   10
   Though you are a Pontic pine,
    daughter of a noble forest,

and boast your useless ancestry and name,
the frightened sailor puts no trust
   in painted sterns. Keep a look out,
      unless you mean to give the winds some sport.

Not long ago you were a worry and a weariness for me,
and now a longing and a deep love.
   So steer clear of the waters that swirl
      between the shining Cyclades.   20

XV

Pastor cum traheret

When the shepherd was dragging Helen off across the sea
on Idaean ships, a traitor carrying off the wife of his host,
Nereus subdued the swift winds and made them idle
   against their will while he sang

his grim prophecies: 'With an ill omen you take home a woman
whom Greece will reclaim with a great army,
swearing an alliance to break your marriage
   and the ancient kingdom of Priam.

Alas! Alas! for the sweat of horses and of men
and for all the deaths you bring to the people of Dardanus.   10
Pallas is already preparing her helmet and aegis,
   her chariot, and the madness of war.

Proud in the protection of Venus, in vain
will you comb your locks and set lovely songs
for ladies to your unwarlike lyre.
   In vain will you hide in your bedchamber

to avoid the heavy spears and the barbs
of Cretan arrows, the din of battle, and the speed
of Ajax's pursuit. But too late, alas! will you smear
   your adulterous hair in the dust.   20

Have you no thought for the son of Laertes, the doom
of your people? For Nestor of Pylos?

Pressing you hard are fearless Teucer of Salamis,
    and Sthenelus, expert in battle

and no sluggard if there is a call to drive a chariot.
Meriones too you will come to know. See there,
raging to find you is the fierce son of Tydeus,
    a better man than his father.

When you see him, like a cowardly stag seeing a wolf
on the other side of the hill, you will forget the grass   30
and run away with your head in the air—
    this is not what you promised your mate.

The anger of Achilles' fleet will postpone
the day of doom for Troy and the women of Phrygia.
After a fixed number of years Achaean fire
    will burn the houses of Ilium.

XVI

O matre pulchra

Daughter lovelier than your lovely mother,
put an end to those scurrilous iambics
    however you wish, whether in the fire
        or in the Adriatic sea.

Neither the goddess of Dindymus, nor the dweller in Delphi
so shakes the minds of the priests in their shrines,
    neither Liber nor the Corybantes so violently
        twin their shrill bronzes

as does intemperate anger. The sword of Noric steel
does not deter it, nor ship-shattering sea,   10
    nor raging fire, nor Jupiter himself
        rushing down in fearful tumult.

They say Prometheus had to add to the primeval slime
a particle cut from each of the animals,
    and grafted the violence of rabid lions
        on to our stomachs.

Anger laid Thyestes low in a heavy doom
and stands as the final cause by which
    lofty cities were razed to the ground,
        and insolent armies drove the plough   20

down on the walls of their enemies.
Subdue your mind. I too was assailed by the fire
    of passion in my breast in the sweet days
        of youth and driven raging

to swift iambics. I now wish to change
from harshness to gentleness, if only,
    my insults now recanted, you become my friend,
        and give me back your heart.

XVII

Velox amoenum

Swift Faunus often exchanges Lycaeus
for my lovely Lucretilis and never fails
    to keep the fiery heat and rainy winds
        from my kidlings.

The wives of stinking billy straggle all over
my wood in perfect safety, looking for
    thyme and arbutus, and the kids
        are never frightened

by green snakes nor the wolves of Mars
whenever the valleys and smooth rocks   10
    on the slopes of Ustica ring, O Tyndaris,
        with the sweet pipe of Faunus.

The gods are guarding me. My piety and my Muse
are near to their hearts. Here for you a rich abundance
    of the glories of the countryside will pour
        from the full horn of plenty.

Here in my sequestered valley you will escape
the heat of the Dogstar, and sing to the Teian lyre
    of Penelope and sea-green Circe,
        both suffering over one man.   20

Here in the shade you will drink cups
of harmless Lesbian wine. Semele's son, Thyonian Bacchus,
    will not join with Mars to stir up battles
        and you will not have to be afraid

of the suspicions of that hot-head Cyrus. He will not
lay a hand on you in passion—a hand too strong to resist—
    or tear the garland plaited in your hair
        or the dress that does not deserve such treatment.

XVIII

Nullam, Vare, sacra

Plant no tree, Varus, before the sacred vine
in the kindly soil round Tibur and the walls of Catilus.
For god has put nothing but obstacles in the way of sober
        men,
and wine is the only thing that puts biting cares to flight.

After wine who harps on about the harshness of soldiering or
        poverty?
Who does not rather speak of father Bacchus and lovely
        Venus?
The fatal brawl of Lapiths and Centaurs over unmixed wine
gives warning that no man should go beyond the rituals

of moderate Liber. Euhius too gives warning, scourge of
        Thracians
when in their greedy lust they draw too fine a line   10
between right and wrong. I will not shake you, fair Bassareus,
against your will, nor will I drag out into the light of day

what is screened by your various leaves. Keep in check
your Berecyntian horn, your wild drums, and your retinue
of blind Self-love, Vainglory raising her empty head absurdly
        high,
and Trust betrayed, squandering secrets, more transparent
        than glass.

XIX

Mater saeva cupidinum

The cruel mother of Desires,
Theban Semele's boy, Bacchus, and amorous Licence
    order me to give my heart
to love, long since ended.

Glycera sets me on fire, the sheen
of her fair skin, flawless as Parian marble,
    her delicious naughtiness,
her face so dangerous to look at.

Venus has deserted Cyprus and rushes
upon me with all her force. She will have no talk   10
    of Scythians or of Parthian horsemen
aggressive in retreat, or of anything else bar love.

Put here for me, lads, a piece of living turf,
some greenery for a sacrifice, and incense
    with a bowl of two-year-old wine.
I'll kill a victim and she will come more gently.

XX

Vile potabis

You will drink from plain cups an ordinary Sabine wine
I put into a Greek jar and sealed
with my own hands the day you, Maecenas,
    knight of great distinction,

were given such applause in the theatre
that the banks of the river of your fathers
and the playful echo from the Vatican Mount
    joined in your praises.

You can drink your Caecuban and the grape
tamed in the Calenian press: 10
no Falernian vines or Formian hills
    soften my wine.

XXI

Dianam tenerae

Sing, tender virgins, of Diana.
Sing, boys, of unshorn Cynthius
    and of Latona, dear to the heart
        of highest Jupiter.

You girls, sing of the goddess who delights in rivers
and in all the foliage of trees standing out
    on chilly Algidus or in the dark woods of Erymanthus
        or green Mount Gragus.

You boys, raise Tempe no less often with your praises,
and Delos, birthplace of Apollo,   10
    whose shoulder gleams with his quiver
        and his brother's lyre.

He will drive war with its tears, and famine and pestilence
with their misery, far from the people and from Caesar
    the Princeps, to the Persians and Britons,
        moved by your prayer.

XXII

Integer vitae

The man who is pure of heart and innocent of evil
needs no Moorish spears, Fuscus,
nor bow nor quiver heavy
    with poison arrows

whether he is setting out across
the sultry Syrtes or inhospitable

Caucasus or lands licked
   by the fabled Hydaspes.

As I wandered far from my farm
in Sabine forest singing of my Lalage   10
without a care to burden me, a wolf ran away from me,
   unarmed as I was—

such a monster as warrior Daunia
does not feed in her broad oak-woods,
nor does the land of Juba, dry nurse of lions,
   bring it to birth.

Set me on barren plains
where no summer breeze revives a tree,
in a zone of the earth oppressed by clouds
   and a hostile Jupiter;   20

set me under the very chariot wheels of the sun
in a land where no man can build a home—
I shall love my Lalage sweetly laughing,
   sweetly speaking.

XXIII

Vitas inuleo

You avoid me, Chloe, like a fawn looking for its mother
who has run off in fright into the trackless mountains,
      and it panics for no good reason
         at the breeze in the wood.

Whether the fluttering leaves of the thorn tree
shudder in the wind or green lizards
      part the brambles, it trembles,
         heart and knees.

Yet I am no man-eating tiger or Gaetulian lion
hunting you down to crunch your bones.   10
      It is time to stop going with your mother.
         You are ready for a man.

XXIV

Quis desiderio

Why should our grief for a man so loved
know any shame or limit? Teach us sad songs,
Melpomene. Your father gave you a clear voice
    and with it the lyre.

So a sleep that will not end bears down
upon Quintilius. Honour, incorruptible Honesty,
sister of Justice, and naked Truth—
    when will they ever see his equal?

Many good men will weep at his death,
but none weep more than you, Virgil. You ask the gods   10
for Quintilius, but your piety counts for nothing.
    They did not give him on such terms.

What if you were to tune a sweeter lyre than Thracian Orpheus
and trees came to listen? Would blood come back
into the empty shade which Mercury has once herded
    into his black flock

with fearful crook? Prayers do not easily
persuade him to open the gates of death.
It is hard. But, by enduring, we can make lighter
    what the gods forbid us to change.   20

XXV

Parcius iunctas

The young bloods are not so eager now
to rattle your closed shutters with volleys of pebbles
and disturb your sleep. The door that once
    moved so very easily

on its hinges, now hugs the threshold.
Less and less often do you hear the cry 'I'm yours,
and dying for your love, Lydia, night after long night,
    and you lie there sleeping.'

Your turn will come, when you are an old rag
in some lonely alley-way, weeping at the insolence of lovers
as the wind from Thrace holds wilder and wilder orgies   11
    between the old moon and the new,

and your burning love, the lust
that drives the mothers of horses to madness,
rages round your ulcerous liver.
    There will be no shortage of complaints

about cheerful youngsters who take
more pleasure in green ivy and dark myrtle,
and dedicate dry leaves to the east wind,
    winter's crony.   20

XXVI

Musis amicus

As a friend of the Muses I shall throw gloom and fear
to the wild winds to carry off to the Cretan sea.
    Little care I what king is causing alarm
        on some icebound northern shore

or what is terrifying Tiridates. You who delight
in pure fountains, sweet Pimpleis, weave flowers
    grown in the sun, weave
        a garland for my friend Lamia.

Without you the honours I confer are worthless.
To sanctify this Lamia with a new lyre   10
    and the plectrum of Lesbos—there is a task
        worthy of you and worthy of your sisters.

XXVII

Natis in usum

—Cups are made for joy. Only Thracians use them
for fighting. Put a stop to this barbarous practice.

Bacchus is a respectable god. Keep him well away
    from brawling and bloodshed.

Wine and lamplight don't belong in the same world
as that Persian dagger. Moderate
    your unholy noise, friends,
        and keep the weight on the elbow.

—You want me to join you in that grim Falernian?
—Let's hear from Megilla's brother from Opys.   10
    What's this wound he's lucky enough to have?
        What's this arrow he's dying from?

—You're hanging back? No more drink
for me. These are my terms. Whatever Venus
    has you in her power, there's no need to blush
        about your burning passion. Your lovers

are always well-born. Whatever it is, come, tell me
your secret. It's safe with me.—Oh you poor devil!
    What a Charybdis you've been caught in! You poor boy!
        You deserve a better flame than that.   20

What witch can free you? What Thessalian magician
with his potions? What god? Not even Pegasus
    will find it easy to disentangle you from the coils
        of that triple Chimaera.

XXVIII

Te maris et terrae

Measurer of earth and ocean and numberless sand,
        Archytas, you are now confined
near the Matine shore, by a little handful of dust duly sprinkled,
        and it profits you nothing to have probed

the dwellings of air and traversed the round vault of heaven
        with a mind that was to die.
The father of Pelops also died, boon companion of the gods,
        and Tithonus, though carried off into the winds,

and Minos, though admitted to the secrets of the gods.
    Tartarus keeps the son of Panthous,   10
though he was twice sent down to Orcus and called the Trojan
      Age
    as his witness, unfastening his shield to prove

that he had given only flesh and sinew to dark death—
    and in your eyes he was no mean teacher
of truth and of nature. But one night waits for all of us
    and all must walk the path of death, and walk it only
      once.

The Furies give some men over to stern Mars for his games.
    The greedy sea is the death of sailors.
Young and old together, the funerals come thronging.
    Proserpina is merciless and runs away from no man.   20

I, too, was overwhelmed in the Illyrian waves by the south
      wind,
    wild comrade of Orion as he sets.
But you, sailor, do not grudge me a little drifting sand
    for my unburied head and bones.

So, for all the threats of the east wind on the western waves,
    may you be safe when the woods
of Venusia are lashed, and may great profit flow down
    upon you from whatever giver,

from favouring Jupiter and from Neptune, guardian of
      Tarentum.
    Do you not care that you are doing a wrong   30
that will hurt your innocent descendants? It may be
    that a debt of justice and a reward for your pride

are waiting even for you. If you abandon me, my curses will
      not go
    unheard, and no expiation will ever acquit you.
You are in haste, but it would not delay you long. Just throw
    three handfuls of dust and go speeding on your way.

XXIX

Icci, beatis

Iccius, are you now envying the rich treasures
of Arabia, preparing a ruthless campaign
    against kings of Sheba never before subdued,
        and weaving chains

for the fearsome Mede? What barbarian virgin will be
your slave, mourning her bridegroom killed in battle?
    What boy of the court brought up to stretch
        Chinese arrows on the bow of his fathers

will take his place by your cup with rich oils
on his hair? Who would deny that down-rushing rivers   10
    can flow up steep mountains
        and Tiber reverse his course

when you are in such haste to exchange for Spanish
            breastplates
the Socratic school and the works of great Panaetius
    collected from all over the world—
        you promised better things.

XXX

O Venus, regina

Venus, queen of Cnidos and Paphos,
abandon your beloved Cyprus and move
to the lovely shrine of Glycera, who summons you
    with clouds of incense.

Your ardent boy must hurry along with you
and Nymphs and Graces with their girdles loose
and Youth, so uncongenial without you,
    and Mercury.

XXXI

Quid dedicatum

What does the bard ask from Apollo whose temple
is now dedicated? What does he pray for
    as he pours the new wine from the bowl? Not
       the fertile crops of wealthy Sardinia,

not the lovely herds of sultry
Calabria, not Indian gold or ivory,
    not land gnawed by the quiet waters
       of the silent river Liris.

Let those to whom Fortune grants it restrain the vine
with the Calenian sickle, and let the rich merchant   10
    drain from golden goblets wine
       bought with Syrian merchandise—

darling of the very gods, visiting
the Atlantic three or four times a year
    and surviving. I eat easily digestible
       olives, chicory, and mallows.

Grant, son of Latona, that I may enjoy what I have
with good health and, I pray, with sound mind,
    and that my old age may not be squalid
       and not without the lyre.   20

XXXII

Poscimus si quid

We pray, if ever we have relaxed with you in the shade
and played a melody that may live a year
    or more, come, my Greek lyre,
       and sound a Latin song.

You were first tuned by a citizen of Lesbos,
fierce in war, who, whether he was where the steel
was flying or had tied up his battered ship
    on the spray-soaked shore,

would still sing of Bacchus and the Muses,
of Venus and the boy who is always by her side,   10
and of Lycus with his jet-black eyes
    and jet-black hair.

O glory of Phoebus, lyre welcome at the feasts
of Supreme Jupiter, O sweet easer of my labours,
grant me your blessing whenever
    I duly call upon you.

XXXIII

Albi, ne doleas

Do not grieve, Albius, remembering too well
your bitter-sweet Glycera and do not keep chanting
piteous elegies wondering why she has broken faith
    and a younger man now outshines you.

Love for Cyrus scorches the beautiful,
narrow-browed Lycoris; Cyrus leans lovingly
over hard-hearted Pholoe, but sooner will roe-deer
    mate with Apulian wolves

than Pholoe soil herself with a foul adulterer.
Such is the decree of Venus, who decides in cruel jest   10
to join unequal minds and bodies
    under her yoke of bronze.

I myself once, when a better love was offered me,
was shackled in the delicious fetters of Myrtale,
a freedwoman wilder than the Adriatic sea
    scooping out the bays of Calabria.

XXXIV

Parcus deorum cultor

I used to worship the gods grudgingly,
and not often, a wanderer expert

in a crazy wisdom, but now I am forced
    to sail back and once again go over

the course I had left behind. For Jupiter
who usually parts the clouds with the fire
    of his lightning has driven his horses
        and his flying chariot across a cloudless sky,

shaking the dull earth and winding rivers,
the Styx and the fearsome halls of hateful Taenarus,   10
    and the Atlantean limits
        of the world. God has the power

to exchange high and low, to humble the great,
and bring forward the obscure. With a shrill cry
    rapacious Fortune snatches the crown from one head
        and delights to lay it on another.

XXXV

O diva, gratum

Goddess, who rule over lovely Antium,
whose present power can raise mortal man
    from the lowest level or turn
        his proud triumphs into funerals,

the poor farmer appeals to you with anxious prayer,
the sailor vexing the Carpathian sea
    on his Bithynian ship prays to you
        as mistress of the ocean.

The rough Dacian and Scythian famous in retreat,
cities and peoples and fierce Latium,   10
    the mothers of barbarian kings
        and tyrants clad in purple,

all are afraid that your violent foot may kick over
the standing column, that the mob may gather
    to whip laggards to war, to war,
        and shatter all authority.

Always before you goes your slave Necessity,
beam-nails and wedges in her bronze hand,
    and never without her cruel hook
        and molten lead.   20

Hope attends you, and Loyalty, rare upon this earth,
her hand swathed in white. They do not desert their friend
    when you change your coat
        and leave the homes of the great.

Then too the faithless mob and lying prostitute
fall away, and false friends, not to be trusted
    to share the yoke, disappear
        when all the jars are drained to the dregs.

Preserve Caesar as he prepares to go
to remotest Britain, and preserve the new swarm   30
    of warriors to spread fear in the regions
        of the East and the Red Sea.

Shame on our scars, our crimes,
our brothers! Our brutal age has shrunk
    from nothing. We have left no impiety
        untouched. Our young men have never

stayed their hand for fear of the gods,
but have polluted every altar. If only
    you would reforge our blunted swords
        to use against Massagetae and Arabs.   40

XXXVI

Et ture et fidibus

With incense and with the lyre
and with the blood of a calf to pay my vow, I delight
    to propitiate the guardian gods
of Numida, now safely home from the furthest West

    and sharing out so many kisses
to his dear friends, but to none

more than his beloved Lamia, remembering
boyhood when none but Lamia was king,

and the time when they both put on the toga.
We must not fail to mark this glorious day with chalk,   10
and the jar we bring out must know no limit
and feet no rest from dancing like the Salii,

nor must Damalis, that great drinker,
down a deeper Thracian draught than Bassus,
nor at this feast must there be any shortage of roses
or long-living celery or soon-dying lilies.

All will fix their melting eyes
on Damalis, and Damalis will not be torn
from the arms of her new lover,
but will wind more clingingly than ivy.   20

XXXVII

Nunc est bibendum

Now we must drink, now we must
beat the earth with unfettered feet, now,
my friends, is the time to load the couches
of the gods with Salian feasts.

Before this it was a sin to take the Caecuban
down from its ancient racks, while the mad queen
with her contaminated flock of men
diseased by vice was preparing

the ruin of the Capitol and the destruction
of our power, crazed with hope   10
unlimited and drunk
with sweet fortune. But her madness

decreased when scarce a ship escaped the flames
and her mind, deranged by Mareotic wine,
was made to face real fears
as she flew from Italy, and Caesar

pressed on the oars (like a hawk
after gentle doves or a swift hunter
   after a hare on the snowy plains
     of Thrace) to put in chains   20

this monster sent by fate. But she looked
for a nobler death. She did not have a woman's fear
   of the sword, nor did she make
     for secret shores with her swift fleet.

Daring to gaze with face serene upon her ruined palace,
and brave enough to take deadly serpents
   in her hand, and let her body
     drink their black poison,

fiercer she was in the death she chose, as though
she did not wish to cease to be a queen, taken to Rome   30
   on the galleys of savage Liburnians,
     to be a humble woman in a proud triumph.

XXXVIII

Persicos odi

I hate Persian luxuries, my boy.
Garlands woven with lime tree bark give me no pleasure.
There's no need for you to seek out
   the last rose where it lingers.

I'm anxious you shouldn't labour
over the simple myrtle. Myrtle suits you
as my cupbearer, and me as I drink
   in the dense shade of the vine.

ODES, BOOK II

I

Motum ex Metello

The civil disturbance which began in the consulship of Metellus
and the causes of the war, its evils and the ways of it,
   the play of Fortune, the fatal friendships
     of the great, and armour

smeared with still unexpiated blood—
themes fraught with the hazard of the dice—
   all these you treat, and tread on fire
     smouldering under ashes.

For a little your strict Tragic Muse must desert
the theatres. In due course, when you have set the affairs   10
   of state in order, you will return to your great duty
     in the buskin of Cecrops,

a glorious bulwark, Pollio, for the abject defendant
and for the Senate consulting you.
   For you the laurel has brought forth honours
     ever green in your Dalmatian triumph.

But now you assault our ears with the menacing thunder
of horns, bugles now blare, the dazzle
   of armour now puts fear into fleeing horses
     and the faces of horsemen.   20

Now I seem to hear of great leaders
begrimed with glorious dust
   and the whole world subdued
     except the fierce spirit of Cato.

Powerless, Juno and all the gods who favour Africa
had abandoned it unavenged,
   but now they have given the descendants of the victors
     as offerings to the shade of Jugurtha.

What field is not fattened with Latin blood,
its graves testifying to impious battles   30
   and the fall of Hesperia
     heard by the Medes?

What sea, what rivers, have not known
this sorry war? What ocean has not been stained
   by the slaughter of Daunians? What shore
     is not soaked with our blood?

But come, my naughty Muse, do not leave
your cheerful ways to take to the duties of Cean dirges.
   Stay with me in Dione's daughter's cave
     and look for measures for a lighter plectrum.   40

II

Nullus argento

Silver has no colour while hidden
in the greedy earth. You are no lover of metal,
Crispus Sallustius, unless it shines
   in tempered use.

Proculeius will live on to distant ages,
renowned for his fatherly feeling for his brothers.
His fame will survive and drive him on with wings
   that scorn to droop.

You can rule a broader kingdom by subduing greed
in your heart than if you were to join Libya   10
to distant Gades, and both Carthages were enslaved
   to you alone.

Dropsy is deadly and it swells by self-indulgence.
You can never drive out the thirst unless the cause of disease
takes flight from the veins and the watery languor
   leaves the pallid body.

Phraates is restored to the throne of Cyrus,
but Virtue dissents from the crowd. She excludes him

from the roll of the blest and teaches the people
    not to use false words.   20

She grants a secure kingdom and diadem
and her own true laurel to that man alone
who sees great wealth heaped up and gives it not
    a backward glance.

III

Aequam memento

Remember to keep your mind level when the path is steep,
and also in prosperity to keep it tempered
    and well away from too much joy, Dellius,
        for you will die

whether you spend every minute of your life in gloom
or bless yourself lying all the long days
    of festivals in secluded meadows
        with Falernian from the back of the cellar.

To what purpose do the huge pine and the white poplar
love to weave their branches into hospitable shade?   10
    And why does the rushing stream twist and strain
        as it bustles along?

Tell them to bring the wine, the fragrant oils,
and the all-too-short-lived flowers of the lovely rose,
    while your age and means and the black threads
        of the three sisters permit.

You will leave the upland pastures you have bought,
You will leave the town house and the country estate
    lapped by the yellow Tiber, and your heir
        will take possession of your high-heaped wealth.   20

It makes no difference whether you spend your time
under the sky as a rich descendant of ancient Inachus
    or whether you are a pauper, the lowest of the low—
        you are the victim of Orcus and he pities no one.

We are all gathered to the same place. All our lots
are turning in the urn, and sooner or later
   they will be shaken out, and put us
      on the boat for an exile that never ends.

IV

Ne sit ancillae

There's no need, Phocian Xanthus, to be ashamed
of your love for a slave girl. Arrogant Achilles
was moved ere now by the white skin of Briseis,
   and she was a slave.

The beauty of captive Tecmessa moved Ajax,
son of Telamon, and he was her master.
In his hour of triumph the son of Atreus burned
   for the maid who was ravished

when the barbarian squadrons fell before
the Thessalian victor and the removal of Hector   10
made it a lighter task for the weary Greeks
   to raze Troy to the ground.

For all you know golden-haired Phyllis
has wealthy parents, a credit to any son-in-law.
The family, no doubt of it, is royal and mourns
   its gods who have turned against it.

You mustn't imagine that such a beloved
comes from the gutter, or that one so faithful,
so unmercenary, could have a mother
   to be ashamed of.   20

I praise her arms, her face, her exquisite ankles,
but am immune. Don't for a moment suspect
a man when time has run away
   with his fortieth year.

V

Nondum subacta

She's not broken in yet and her neck hasn't the strength
to bear the yoke. She can't pull
    with a partner or bear the weight
        of an amorous bull plunging into love.

That young heifer of yours has her mind
on grassy meadows, finding relief from the sultry heat
    in rivers, or longing to play precocious games
        with bullocks

in willow marshes. Give up your desire
for the unripe grape. Autumn will soon mark out   10
    the blue clusters for you,
        tinging them with his purple.

She'll soon be after you. Time runs
mercilessly on and will give to her the years
    it takes from you. Lalage will soon be butting
        her mate with lusty forehead

and be loved more than the runaway Pholoe,
more than Chloris, whose white shoulder gleams
    like the pure moon glinting on the night sea,
        more than Cnidian Gyges.   20

Put him in a dance with girls
and the nice distinction would wonderfully deceive
    your most perceptive guests—
        that flowing hair and that ambiguous face.

VI

Septimi, Gades aditure

You who would go with me to Gades, Septimius,
to the Cantabrian, who has never learned to bear our yoke,
or to the barbarian Syrtes, where the Moorish sea
    for ever boils,

let Tibur, founded by the settler from Argos,
be the resting-place of my old age. Weary as I am,
let it be the end of sea and roads
    and soldiering.

But if the cruel Fates keep me from Tibur,
I shall make for the sweet waters of the Galaesus   10
with its leather-coated sheep, and the country kingdom
    once ruled by Laconian Phalanthus.

This, above all others, is the corner of the earth
that smiles for me, where the honey does not yield
to Hymettus and the olive challenges
    green Venafrum,

where Jupiter gives a long spring
and warm winters, and the Aulon valley is a friend
to fertile Bacchus, envying not in the least
    the grapes of Falernum.   20

This is the place that calls out to you and me.
These are the blest citadels. There you will sprinkle
the tear you owe on the warm ashes
    of your friend the bard.

VII

O saepe mecum

You and I, Pompeius, have often been led
to the edge of doom when Brutus was our commander.
    Who has given you back as a Roman citizen
        to the gods of your fathers and the skies of Italy?

Pompeius, first of my friends, many's the time
we have broken into the lingering day with neat wine,
    heads garlanded and hair sleek
        with Syrian ointment.

With you I learned all about Philippi and speedy flight,
and shamefully left my little shield behind   10
    when virtue snapped and the chins of blusterers
        touched the dirt of the earth.

But swift Mercury came to me in my panic and
carried me in a dense mist through the enemy ranks,
    while a wave sucked you back into war
        and swept you along in the boiling straits.

So pay to Jupiter the feast you owe him,
under my laurel lay down your body
    worn out by long campaigning, and have no mercy
        on the casks I have laid down for you.   20

Fill up the polished Egyptian cups with Massic wine
for forgetfulness, and pour the fragrant oils
    from huge conches. Who is responsible
        for hurrying up garlands of moist parsley

and of myrtle? Who will throw a Venus and become king
of the wine? I shall run as wild as any Edonian
    at her Bacchic orgies. My friend is back.
        What joy to go mad!

VIII

Ulla si iuris

If you had ever suffered any punishment
for perjury, Barine, if you were uglier
by one black tooth or by a speck of white
    on a fingernail,

I would be a believer. But the minute you pledge
your perfidious self, your beauty is enhanced
and you walk the streets a public menace
    to young men.

It has paid you to swear false oaths by the ashes of your mother
in her tomb, by the silent stars of night, sky and all,   10
and by the gods who never feel
    the chill of death.

Venus herself, I do declare, laughs at this,
the guileless nymphs laugh at it, and heartless Cupid,

for ever sharpening burning arrows
   on a whetstone dripping with blood.

Add to the case that all the young grow into your love,
new slaves arrive to swell the troop, and the old ones
never leave the house of their impious mistress,
   for all their threats.   20

Mothers are afraid of you for the sake
of their young bullocks, close-fisted old men too,
and new brides in case their husbands catch your scent
   and come home late.

IX

Non semper imbres

Rain is not always streaming down from the clouds
on roughened fields, wild squalls
   are not for ever vexing the Caspian sea,
      and not through every month of the year,

my dear friend Valgius, does the ice stand motionless
on the shores of Armenia, nor do the oaks of Garganus
   labour in north winds nor are ash trees
      always being widowed of their leaves.

But you are always harassing your lost lover Mystes
with mournful melodies and your love never leaves you,   10
   not when Vesper rises
      nor when he retreats from the scorching sun.

But the old man who lived three lifetimes did not spend
all his years in mourning for his beloved Antilochus,
   and the Trojan parents and sisters
      of young Troilus did not always

weep for him. The time has come to give over
these soft complaints. Let us rather sing
   of the new trophies of Caesar Augustus,
      of the Niphates frozen hard,   20

of the Persian river joining its peoples in defeat
and lowering the crests of its rolling waves,
    of the Geloni in their reservation
        riding their horses in their narrow plains.

X

Rectius vives

You will take a better course, Licinius,
if you do not always thrust over the deep sea,
or hug the dangerous coast too close,
    shivering at the prospect of squalls.

Whoever loves the Golden Mean
is safe (no squalor for him in a filthy garret),
and temperate (for him no mansion
    that men will envy).

The huge pine is more cruelly tossed
by the winds, the loftiest towers   10
have the heaviest fall and lightning strikes
    the tops of mountains.

The heart well prepared hopes in adversity
for a change in fortune, and fears it in prosperity.
Jupiter brings back ugly winters
    and Jupiter

removes them. If all goes badly now, some day
it will not be so. Sometimes Apollo rouses
the silent Muse with his lyre. He does not always
    stretch his bow.   20

In difficult straits show spirit
and courage, and when the wind
is too strong at your back, be wise
    and shorten the bulging sail.

XI

Quid bellicosus

Do not trouble to ask, Quinctius, my dear Hirpanian friend,
what the war-loving Cantabrian is thinking, or the Scythian
   —he's kept well away by the barrier of the Adriatic—
     and stop worrying about the needs of life.

Life asks so little. Smooth-faced youth
and beauty run away behind us.
   When our hair is dry and grey, that puts an end
     to love's pleasures and easy sleep.

The glory of spring flowers is not for ever constant.
The blushing moon does not always shine   10
   with the same face. Why weary your little mind
     with eternal thoughts?

Why do we not lie down under a tall plane tree,
or here without more ado under this pine,
   and drink, while we may, our grey heads
     perfumed with roses and anointed

with Assyrian nard? Euhius dispels
all gnawing cares. Won't some boy come quickly
   and douse the fire of this Falernian wine
     from the stream flowing by?   20

Will someone tempt Lyde from her secluded home?
Go on, tell her to hurry and bring
   her ivory lyre, tying her uncombed hair
     in a knot in the Spartan style.

XII

Nolis longa ferae

Long wars in fierce Numantia, Hannibal iron-hard,
the Sicilian sea purpled with Punic blood—
   you would not wish these themes set
     to the soft measures of the lyre,

nor savage Lapiths, nor Hylaeus ungovernable
in his cups, nor the defeat at the hand of Hercules
of the warrior sons of earth, whose threats
    shook the gleaming house

of old Saturn. You will do better yourself, Maecenas,
by speaking in prose histories of Caesar's battles   10
and menacing kings dragged through the streets
    by their necks.

As for me, the Muse has wished that I should speak
of the sweet songs of the lady Licymnia, her eyes
brightly shining, her heart truly faithful
    to a requited love.

She was not disgraced in the chorus of dancers
or contest of wit, or playing arm in arm
with shining maidens in crowded temple
    on Diana's holy day.   20

Surely you would willingly exchange the rich possessions
of Achaemenes, or the wealth of Mygdon
in fat Phrygia, or the full-stocked homes of the Arabs
    for a strand of Licymnia's hair

when she bends down her neck to burning kisses,
or cruelly teases by refusing them, though she enjoys
stolen kisses more than the one who asks for them,
    and sometimes is quick to steal them herself.

XIII

Ille et nefasto

Not only did he plant you on an unholy day,
whoever did it first, but he also tended you
    with sacrilegious hand—a tree to destroy
      his descendants and disgrace the district,

and I could believe he strangled his own father
and spattered one night the shrine of the gods
    of his house with the blood of a guest.
        He dealt in Colchian poisons

and every crime devised in every corner
of the world—the man who planted you in my field,   10
    you evil timber, set to fall
        on your innocent master's head.

No man can ever see for sure from hour to hour
what he should avoid. The Phoenician sailor shudders
    at the Bosphorus and, clear of the straits, fails
        to see death coming from some other quarter.

The soldier is afraid of arrows and the Parthian's swift flight.
The Parthian fears chains and a Roman dungeon,
    but no man foretells the stroke of death which has carried off
        the peoples of the earth, and always will.   20

How nearly did we see the kingdom
of dark Proserpina, and Aeacus in judgement,
    and the seats of the holy set apart,
        and Sappho complaining

of her young countrywomen to her Aeolian lyre,
and you, Alcaeus, sounding in fuller tones
    with your golden plectrum the rigours of shipboard,
        the cruel rigours of exile, the rigours of war.

The shades listen in wonderment and sacred silence
to the words of both, but with more willing ear   30
    the crowd packed shoulder to shoulder drinks in
        battles and expulsions of tyrants.

Little wonder, when the hundred-headed monster,
struck dumb by the singing, lets down his black ears,
    and coiling snakes come to life
        in the hair of the Furies.

Even Prometheus and the father of Pelops
are cheated of their labour by the sweet music.
    and Orion neglects to drive the lions
        and the timorous lynxes.   40

XIV

Eheu fugaces

Ah how quickly, Postumus, Postumus,
the years glide by, and piety will not delay
    the wrinkles, and old age, and death, the unsubdued,
        pressing at their heels,

no, my friend, not if every day that passes you sacrificed
three hundred bulls to appease Pluto, the god
    who cannot weep, who confines Tityos
        and the three-bodied giant Geryon

in the prison of those gloomy waters
that we know all of us must cross   10
    who feed upon the bounty of the earth,
        whether we be kings or poor tenant farmers.

In vain shall we avoid the bloody god of war
and the roaring breakers of the Adriatic.
    In vain autumn after long autumn shall we tremble
        for our health when the south wind blows.

We must go and see black Cocytus meandering
in its sluggish flow, the infamous daughters of Danaus,
    and Sisyphus, son of Aeolus,
        at his long sentence of hard labour.   20

We must leave the earth, our home,
and the wife we love, and none of these trees you tend
    except the hated cypresses
        will go with their short-lived master.

Your heir, worthier than yourself, will drink off
the Caecuban you laid down behind a hundred locks,
    and stain your paving with proud wine undiluted
        and too good for the banquets of priests.

XV

Iam pauca aratro

Huge palaces will soon leave few acres
for the plough. On every side fishpools
   broader than the Lucrine lake
     will meet the eye and the bachelor plane

will push out the elm. Then myrtles and beds of violet
and everything the nose could desire
   will then sprinkle perfumes where the old farmer
     had his fertile olive groves.

The dense laurel will then block the fiery shafts
of the sun. This is not what was prescribed by the auspices
   taken by Romulus and bearded Cato   11
     and by the rule of the ancients.

Their private wealth was small.
Their public wealth was great. No portico laid out
   by ten-foot rod caught the dense northern shade
     for private citizens.

The laws commanded them not to despise the turf
beneath their feet, but to beautify at common cost
   their towns and the temples of their gods
     with freshly quarried stone.   20

XVI

Otium divos

The man caught in the open Aegean asks the gods
for peace of mind, as soon as a dark cloud obscures
the moon and stars no longer shine
   to give sure guidance to sailors.

'Peace of mind,' asks Thrace so furious in war.
'Peace of mind,' cry the Medes with their gorgeous quivers.
But peace cannot be bought with jewels, Grosphus,
   nor with purple or gold.

No treasure and no consul's lictor
disperse the riots of a troubled mind   10
or the cares fluttering
    round coffered ceilings.

A man lives well on little if his father's salt-cellar
shines on his modest table,
and if fear and sordid greed do not disturb
    his easy sleep.

Why do we brave fellows throw so many javelins
in our short lives? Why travel to places
warmed by a different sun? What exile
    has ever escaped himself?   20

Corroding care boards the bronze-prowed ship.
It rides with squadrons of horsemen.
It is swifter than deer, swifter than the east wind
    driving the clouds.

The mind which finds delight in the present moment
should not worry about what is to come,
but should dilute all bitterness with a slow smile.
    Nothing is perfect in every part.

An early death carried off the glorious Achilles,
a long old age reduced Tithonus,   30
and time will perhaps hold out to me
    what it denies to you.

Round you are lowing a hundred herds
of Sicilian cattle. For you is neighing the mare
fit for a four-horse chariot. You are clad
    in wool twice dyed

by African shellfish. To me Fate, untreacherous,
has given a small farm and the modest breath
of a Greek Camena and allowed me to despise
    the malice of the mob.   40

XVII

Cur me querelis

Why do you frighten me to death with your moaning?
It's no wish of the gods or of myself that you should die
    before me, Maecenas, my crowning glory
        and roof-tree of my house.

Come! If some blow strikes you first and carries off
the half of my life, what is there to keep
    the other half here? I like it less,
        the damaged half. That day

will bring ruin to both of us. I have taken my oath
and will not be false to it. We shall go, yes,   10
    we shall go whenever you take the lead, comrades
        ready to take the last road together.

Not the fiery breath of the Chimaera,
not hundred-handed Gyges if he rose again,
    will ever tear me from your side. Such is the decree
        of mighty justice and the Fates.

Whether Libra turns its aspect on me
or terrifying Scorpio, the more violent part
    of my horoscope, or Capricorn,
        the tyrant of the western wave,   20

our two stars are in wondrous conjunction.
Your protector Jupiter blazed back
    at impious Saturn and rescued you,
        slowing the swift wings

of Fate when the people in the crowded theatre
three times gave their glad applause;
    as for me, the tree would have fallen on my head
        and carried me off if Faunus,

the guardian of Mercury's men, had not parried
the blow with his right hand. Do not omit   30
    to offer sacrifices and build a votive temple;
        we will kill a little lamb.

XVIII

Non ebur neque aureum

Neither ivory nor gold-coffered
ceiling gleams in my house,
    nor do beams from Mount Hymettus
bear down on columns hewn in furthest

Africa, nor am I the unknown heir
of Attalus come to take over his palace,
    nor do distinguished women clients
trail their robes of Laconian purple for me,

but I have honesty and a generous vein
of talent and though I am poor, I am courted   10
    by the rich. I do not trouble the gods
for more or solicit a powerful friend

   for greater gifts, being blest enough
with the one and only Sabine country.
    Day treads on day,
new moons are quick to perish,

while you place contracts for cutting marble
and building homes just before your funeral
    with never a thought of your tomb, and struggle
to push back the shore of the sea   20

which roars at Baiae's beach,
thinking yourself a pauper because you are confined to land.
    Yet all the time you tear up
your neighbours' boundary-stones

and leap over your clients' walls
in your greed. Husband and wife
    are driven out carrying in their arms
their fathers' gods and their mourning children.

But no palace more surely
awaits the rich landowner   30
    than the end rapacious Orcus
has destined for him. Why struggle to go further?

The same amount of earth
opens for the poor man and for the sons of kings,
    and gold could not suborn
the steward of Orcus to untie ingenious Prometheus.

He confines proud Tantalus
and the lineage of Tantalus. He relieves
    the poor man when his toil is over
and hears him, whether called or not.   40

XIX

Bacchum in remotis

I have seen Bacchus among the lonely crags,
teaching songs—believe me, generations yet unborn—
    and Nymphs learning them, and goat-footed Satyrs
      pricking up their ears.

Euhoe! My breast is full of Bacchus. My mind
thrills with the terror I have seen and wildly rejoices.
    Euhoe! Spare me, Liber, spare me,
      fearful with your irresistible thyrsus.

It is no sin for me to sing of your wilful Thyiades,
and your fountain of wine, of rich rivers   10
    of milk, and again and again of honey
      dripping from hollow tree trunks.

Nor is it a sin to sing of the honour accorded
to your blessed wife now added to the stars, the palace
    of Pentheus pitilessly torn to shreds,
      and the doom of Thracian Lycurgus.

You change the course of rivers, you curb the barbarian sea,
and drenched with wine on distant ridges
    you bind the hair of Bistonian women
      in knots of harmless vipers.   20

When the impious army of Giants scaled
the heights of your father's kingdom,

you hurled Rhoetus back
    with your fearful lion's jaws and claws.

They said you were fitter for dance
and jest and play, not wholly suited
    to battle, but you were the centre
        of peace and war alike.

Cerberus saw you in all your beauty with your golden horn
and did you no harm but gently brushed his tail   30
    against you and licked your departing feet
        and legs with his three tongues.

XX

Non usitata

This is no ordinary, no flimsy wing which will bear
me, half-bard, half-bird, through the liquid air,
    nor shall I longer remain on the earth,
        but, grown too large for envy, I shall leave

its cities. I, who am of the blood of poor parents,
I, who come at your command,
    my beloved Maecenas, shall not die,
        nor be confined by the waves of the Styx.

Already, even now, rough skin is forming
on my legs, my upper part is changing   10
    into a white swan and smooth feathers
        are sprouting along my fingers and shoulders.

Already more famous than Icarus, son of Daedalus,
I shall visit, a harmonious bird, the shores
    of the moaning Bosphorus, the Gaetulian Syrtes,
        and the Hyperborean plains.

The Colchian will know me, and the Dacian who pretends
not to fear a cohort of Marsians, the Geloni
    at the ends of the earth, the learned Iberian,
        the Rhône-swigger.   20

Let there be no dirges or squalid mourning
or lamentation at my corpseless funeral.
  Check your cries of grief and do not trouble
    with the empty honour of a tomb.

ODES, BOOK III

I

Odi profanum vulgus

I hate the profane mob and keep them at a distance.
Maintain a holy silence. As priest of the Muses
   I sing for girls and boys
      songs never heard before.

Dread kings hold sway over their flocks;
over kings rules Jupiter,
   resplendent in triumph over the Giants,
      moving all things with his eyebrow.

One man trenches broader acres for his vines
than his neighbour, one candidate going down to the Campus
   is more nobly born, another competes   11
      in character and reputation,

another has a larger retinue of clients—
Necessity with her impartial law picks out by lot
   both high and humble.
      All names are shaken in that capacious urn.

If the naked sword hangs over your impious neck,
Sicilian banquets will not contrive
   a sweet savour for you.
      Neither the song of birds nor the lyre   20

will bring you sleep. But soothing sleep does not despise
the humble homes of country people,
   the shady river bank, or Tempe's wooded valley
      stirred by western breezes.

The man who wants enough and no more
is not disturbed by stormy seas or the fierce onset
   of the Bearkeeper falling
      or the rising Kid,

not by hail battering his vineyards,
or by his treacherous farm with trees always grumbling   30
   about floods, about stars scorching the fields,
     about cruel winters.

Fish feel the shrinking of the water when massive piers
are dropped into the deep. Here come crowding
   the master who has wearied of dry land
     and the contractor with his slaves throwing in

their building rubble. But Fear and Foreboding
climb as high as the master. Black Care
   stays aboard the bronze-plated trireme,
     and sits behind the Knight.   40

If sorrow is not soothed by Phrygian marble
or the wearing of purple brighter than the purple
   of Sidon, or by Falernian wine
     and the balsam of the Achaemenids,

why should I raise a lofty entrance hall
in a new style with doorposts for all to envy?
   Why should I give up my Sabine valley
     for riches which bring more labour?

II

Angustam amice

The boy must be toughened by hard campaigning and learn
happily to endure the restrictions of poverty,
   riding against fierce Parthians,
     spreading terror with his sword,

and living in danger under the sky. When the maiden
grown to womanhood and the mother
   of the warring king gaze at him
     from the walls of the enemy city,

let them sigh their sighs for the royal bridegroom
new to the ranks, in case he rouse the lion   10

it is death to touch, whose anger whirls him
  in blood through the thick of slaughter.

Sweet it is and honourable to die for one's native land.
Death hunts down even the man who runs away
  and does not spare the back or hamstrings
    of young cowards.

Virtue knows nothing of humiliation at the polls
but shines with honours unsullied. She does not take up
  the axes or lay them down at the breath
    of the wind of popular opinion.   20

Virtue opens a way to heaven for those who deserve
not to die. She dares to take the forbidden path,
  spurning the vulgar throng and the dank earth
    with soaring wing.

For faithful silence, too, there is secure reward.
I will not have under my roof-tree the man
  who blurts out the secret Mysteries of Ceres
    nor will he sail my fragile boat

with me. When Jupiter is neglected he often involves
the pure with the impure. The wicked man goes   30
  on his way, but Punishment rarely deserts him,
    although her foot is lame.

III

Iustum et tenacem

The just man who holds fast to his resolve
is not shaken in firmness of mind by the passion
  of citizens demanding what is wrong,
    or the menace of the tyrant's frown, or the wind

of the south, rebellious king of the unquiet Adriatic,
or by the mighty hand of Jupiter who wields the lightning.
  If the round world were to break and fall about him,
    its ruins would strike him unafraid.

By such arts did Pollux and far-travelled Hercules
prevail and reach the citadels of fire,   10
    and between them Augustus will recline,
        drinking the nectar with his purple lips.

By such arts, Father Bacchus, and by your just deserts,
were you drawn by tigers, bearing the yoke
    on necks untameable. By such arts Romulus Quirinus
        escaped from Acheron on the horses of Mars

after Juno had spoken and the gods in council
had approved: 'Ilium, O Ilium, you were turned
    to dust by the unchaste judge
        and the woman sent by Fate from across the seas.   20

From the moment Laomedon cheated the gods
of promised payment, Ilium was consigned to me
    and to chaste Minerva, and with it the people
        and their lying king.

The Spartan adulteress's notorious visitor
no longer preens himself nor do the oath-breakers
    of the house of Priam beat back the warlike Greeks
        with Hector to give them strength.

The war dragged out by our disputes has now
subsided. In this moment I lay by   30
    my savage anger and give over to Mars
        the grandson I loathed, child

of a Trojan priestess. I shall suffer him to enter
the regions of light, to drink the juice
    of nectar and be enrolled
        among the serene ranks of the gods.

Provided the wide sea rages between Ilium
and Rome, wherever Romans may be
    let them rule and prosper—as exiles.
        Provided the cattle trample   40

the tomb of Priam and of Paris, and the wild beasts safely
hide their litters there, let the Capitol stand gleaming
    and fierce Rome impose her laws
        upon the defeated Medes.

Let her be feared and spread her name
to the furthest shores where the middle sea
    parts Europe from Africa and where
      the swollen Nile irrigates its fields.

And let her be strong to despise gold and leave it
undiscovered in the earth—and better thus   50
    than pressed into the service of man
      whose hand despoils all that is sacred.

Whatever limits are set to our world,
let her reach out to them, eager to go
    where fire and cloud and the dew
      of rain hold their wild orgies.

But I speak this prophecy for the Quirites,
warlike citizens of Rome, on condition that they do not,
    in excess of piety or confidence, decide
      to rebuild their ancestral homes in Troy.   60

Troy's fortunes, if they are reborn
under that ill omen, will once again end in utter disaster,
    and I shall lead the victorious armies,
      the wife of Jupiter and his sister.

If the bronze wall rose again three times and Apollo
built it three times, my Greeks would cut it down,
    three times the captive woman
      would weep for her husband and her sons.'

This will not suit my playful lyre.
Where are you going, obstinate Muse? Stop   70
    retailing the talk of gods and
      reducing great matters to your tiny measures.

IV

Descende caelo

Descend from the sky, Queen Calliope,
come, utter a long melody on the pipe,

or with your piercing voice, if you prefer,
or on the lyre or cithara of Phoebus.

Do you hear? Or does some seductive
madness mock me? I seem to hear you
and to be wandering through sacred groves
visited by gracious winds and waters.

One day when I was a boy on Apulian Vultur,
over the threshold of my nurse, the land of Apulia,   10
I was overcome with sleep and play
and the fabled doves laid on me

a covering of fresh leaves. Great was the wonderment
of all who live in Acheruntia's lofty nest,
and the high Bantine woods, and down
in the rich ploughland of Forentum,

to hear how I slept, unmolested by black vipers
and bears, how sacred laurel and myrtle
were gathered and heaped upon this infant
filled with the inspiration of the gods.   20

I am yours, Camenae, yours as I climb
into the steep Sabine hills or delight in cool
Praeneste or Tibur reclining on its hill
or the waters of Baiae.

I who love your fountains and your dancing choirs
was not dispatched when the line broke at Philippi
nor by the accursed tree
nor by Palinurus in the Sicilian waves.

Whenever you are with me, cheerfully
shall I take ship and brave the raging   30
Bosphorus or go on my travels
to the burning sands of the Assyrian shore.

I shall visit the Britons, cruel to strangers,
and Concanians, swigging their horses' blood,
I shall visit the Geloni with their quivers,
and the Scythian river—and not be harmed.

As soon as high Caesar had hidden away
his war-weary cohorts in the towns
   and was seeking to put an end to his labours,
      you renewed him in your Pierian cave.   40

You, nurturing goddesses, give gentle counsel
and rejoice in it when given. We know
   how the impious Titans and their monstrous crew
      were carried away by the falling thunderbolt

of him who governs dull earth and windy ocean,
who rules alone with just authority
   the gloomy cities and kingdoms of the dead,
      the gods, and the armies of men.

Great was the terror brought to Jupiter
by these warriors trusting in their bristling hands,   50
   these brothers who strove
      to heap Pelion on dark Olympus.

But what could Typhoeus and mighty Mimas do
or Porphyrion for all his threatening stance?
   What could Rhoetus achieve
      or bold Enceladus, by tearing up trees

and charging the sounding aegis
of Pallas Athene? Here against them stood
   the greedy god of fire. Here stood the mother goddess Juno
      and the god who will never take the bow   60

from his shoulder, who washes his flowing hair
in the pure waters of Castalia, who haunts
   the thickets of Lycia and his native wood—
      Apollo of Delos and Patara.

Force without wisdom falls by its own weight.
When force is tempered, the gods also advance it
   and make it greater. They abhor violence,
      which moves all manner of impiety in the heart.

Gyges the hundred-hander is my witness
Well-known also is the infamous Orion,   70
   who assaulted chaste Diana
      and was subdued by the maiden's arrow.

Earth grieves when thrown upon her own monstrous brood,
and mourns her sons sent by the lightning bolt
   to flame-lit Orcus. The swift fire
    has not consumed Mount Etna

laid upon them, nor does the bird posted to keep watch
over the vileness of insatiable Tityos leave
   his liver. Three hundred chains hold
    in check the adulterer Pirithous.   80

V

Caelo tonantem

Jupiter thunders in the sky, and we have believed
that he rules; Augustus will be held to be a god
   in our midst when Britons and dread Persians
    are added to the empire.

Have soldiers of Crassus lived on as the shameful husbands
of barbarous wives, and have the Marsian and Apulian
   —shame on the Senate and our changed ways—
    grown old bearing arms for their fathers-in-law

and serving the King of the Medes, forgetting
the sacred shields, their own names, the toga,   10
   and eternal Vesta, while Jupiter
    and the city of Rome still live?

This is what the far-seeing mind of Regulus
had been vigilant against, refusing
   a shameful treaty and deducing from this example
    disaster for an age yet to come,

if the young prisoners did not die
unpitied: 'I have seen hanging in the temples
   of Carthage,' he said 'standards and armour
    stripped from our soldiers,   20

and no blood shed. I have seen Roman citizens
with hands tied behind their backs, the gates
   of Carthage open, and fields once ravaged
    by our armies now under cultivation.

If gold ransoms a man, will he come back
a braver soldier? You are adding waste
  to shame. Dyed wool does not regain
    the colours it has lost

and true courage takes care not to return
to men who have been disgraced, If the doe   30
  fights when freed from the nets,
    then the man who has given himself up

to treacherous enemies will be brave, and one
who has meekly felt the thongs gripping his arms
  and been afraid of death, will trample
    Carthaginians underfoot in another war.

These are men who did not know where to find life.
They have mingled peace and war. Oh the shame of it!
  O mighty Carthage, raised upon the ruins
    of Rome disgraced!'   40

They say he refused his chaste wife's kiss
and pushed away his children, as though no longer
  a Roman. He kept his severe
    and manly gaze upon the ground

till his authority could strengthen the wavering senators
by such counsel as had never before been given,
  and then he hastened through his grieving friends
    into glorious exile.

And yet he knew what tortures the barbarian
was preparing for him, as he parted the kinsmen   50
  who blocked his way, and the Roman people
    delaying his return,

as though judgement had been given in a long case
fought on behalf of his dependants
  and he was leaving for the fields of Venafrum
    or for Lacedaemonian Tarentum.

VI

Delicta maiorum

Though innocent, Roman, you will pay for the sins
of your fathers until you restore
    the crumbling temples and shrines of the gods
        and their smoke-blackened images.

You rule because you hold yourself inferior to the gods.
Make this the beginning and the end of all things.
    Neglect of the gods has brought many ills
        to the sorrowing land of Hesperia.

Already Monaeses and the army of Pacorus
have twice shattered our attacks made without auspices   10
    and grinning barbarians add Roman loot
        to their paltry neckbands.

Our city, caught up in internal strife,
has been almost destroyed
    by the Ethiopian with his formidable fleet,
        and the Dacian prevailing with his flights of arrows.

Our generation is prolific in evil.
First it has corrupted marriage, family, and home,
    and from that source disaster has flowed
        over our whole land and its people.   20

The young girl thrills to learn the movements
of Ionian dance steps, long moulded to such arts
    by obscene lusts practised
        from tenderest childhood.

Soon, while her husband is in his cups, she is looking out
for younger lovers. It is not her way to select
    a recipient for snatched, illicit pleasures
        in the darkness,

rather does she rise, on invitation, before the eyes
of her conniving husband, if a salesman   30
    or Spanish sea captain calls for her
        and pays a good price for her shame.

Not from such parents sprang the men
who stained the sea with Punic blood
    and cut down Pyrrhus, mighty Antiochus
        and the deadly Hannibal.

These were the manly sons of farmer soldiers
and their skill was to turn the sod
    with Sabine mattocks and carry the wood
        they had cut under the command   40

of a strict mother as the sun moved round
the mountain shadows, loosing the weary oxen
    from the yoke when its chariot
        brought on the hour they longed for.

What has injurious time not diminished?
Our parents were not the men their fathers were,
    and they bore children worse than themselves,
        whose children will be baser still.

VII

Quid fles, Asterie

Why weep, Asterie, for someone the fresh winds
of the west will bring back to you at first spring
    with a rich cargo from Thynia,
        a young man constant and true,

your Gyges? The She-goat rose in her fury
and the southerlies drove him into Oricum,
    where he spends cold sleepless nights,
        weeping many a tear.

Yet the messenger comes from his host's wife—
Chloe is unhappy, sighing her heart out, burning   10
    with passion for the man you love—
        the cunning rogue tempts him a thousand ways.

He tells of the lying woman
whose false accusations drove trusting Proetus
    to speed the death
        of all-too-chaste Bellerophon.

He tells the story of Peleus, almost sent down to Hades
for chastely resisting Hippolyte of Magnes,
    and spins lying tales
        to teach him to do wrong—   20

In vain. Deafer than the rocks on the Icarian sea,
he hears, and still is true. But as for you,
    be careful. Do not let your neighbour Enipeus
        charm you more than he ought.

Although on the Campus Martius you will see
nobody so adept at managing a horse
    and nobody swimming so fast
        down Tiber's course,

lock up your house when it begins to get dark,
don't look down into the street when you hear   30
    a plaintive pipe, and when he calls you cruel,
        keep on resisting.

VIII

Martiis caelebs

What am I, a bachelor, doing on the first of March?
What are the flowers for, the censer full
of incense, and the charcoal on the living turf?
   Are you surprised,

you, a scholar of dialogues in both languages?
The day on which I was almost sent to my tomb
by a blow from a tree, I vowed to Liber
   a delicious feast and a white goat.

As the year comes round, this is the day
that will open the cork sealed with pitch   10
in the amphora taught to drink the smoke
   when Tullus was consul.

Drink a hundred ladles, Maecenas, to the escape
of your friend and keep the lamps awake
till the light of dawn. Here let there be
   no shouting or anger.

Lay aside your cares for the city and the citizens,
the army of Cotiso the Dacian is wiped out,
the Medes are their own enemies, divided
    in a bloody civil war,   20

the Cantabrian, our ancient foe on the Spanish shore,
is subdued and in chains at last, the Scythians
have now unstrung their bows and are preparing
    to leave their plains.

Don't trouble to ask where the Roman people is in trouble.
You are a private citizen, spare your worries,
take the gifts of this present hour, and enjoy them.
    Leave serious matters behind you.

IX

Donec gratus eram

—'While I was still attractive to you
and there was no better man to put his arms
    round your white neck,
I was more blest than the king of Persia.'

—'While you did not yet burn with love
for another woman and Lydia did not come second to Chloe,
    the famous Lydia
was more glorious than Roman Ilia.'

—'Now it is Thracian Chloe who rules me,
expert in sweet measures, skilled in the lyre,   10
    I shall not be afraid to die for her
if the Fates spare my beloved's life.'

—'It is Calais, son of Ornytus of Thurii,
for whom I burn and who burns for me.
    I shall endure to die twice for him
if the Fates spare my boy's life.'

—'What if the old Venus returns and forces
those who have been parted to join under her yoke of bronze,
      if golden Chloe is pushed out
and the door stands open for Lydia who was rejected?'   20

—'Although he is lovelier than a star
and you bob about like a cork and are worse-tempered
      than the surly Adriatic,
I would love to live with you and with you I would gladly
      die.'

X

Extremum Tanain

If you were drinking the waters of the distant Don, Lyce,
and married to a barbarous husband, you would still be sorry
to make me lie here on your cruel doorstep at the mercy
      of your neighbours the north winds.

Do you hear your door creaking, and the trees
in your lovely courtyard groaning at the winds,
and Jupiter in a clear sky
      freezing the fallen snow?

Venus does not like pride. Lay it aside,
or the rope will run back with the wheel.   10
Your Etruscan father did not bear a Penelope
      to resist all suitors.

Though you are not moved by gifts or prayers
or the violet tinge of a lover's pallor
or your husband's infatuation with that woman
      from Pieria, come, take pity

on your suppliants. You are no softer than unbending oak,
nor more kindly-minded than Moorish serpents.
This body of mine will not for ever endure your doorstep
      and these waters from heaven.   20

XI

Mercuri—nam te

I call upon you, Mercury—you were the master who taught
your pupil Amphion to move stones by singing—
and upon you, tortoise, so adept
    to make the seven strings sound.

Once dumb and graceless, now you are welcome
at the tables of the rich and in the temples of the gods,
come, strike up measures to catch
    the obstinate ears of Lyde,

cavorting on the broad plains like a two-year-old foal,
afraid to be touched, knowing nothing   10
of marriage, still unmounted
    by a passionate mate.

You can draw tigers and woods in your train,
and check the flow of swift rivers. The watchdog
of the monstrous kingdom, Cerberus himself,
    yielded to your charms,

though his head, like a Fury's,
is set about by a hundred snakes,
and foul breath and gore oozes
    from his triple-tongued mouth.   20

Even Ixion and Tityos forced their faces
into smiles and the urn stood dry for a moment,
while your sweet singing beguiled
    the daughters of Danaus.

Let Lyde hear of their crime and also
of its famous punishment, the vat of water for ever
emptying through a leaking bottom,
    and the fate that awaits

sinners in the end, even in the Underworld.
These wicked girls—what crime could be greater?—   30
these wicked girls could take cold steel
    to their new husbands.

One of the many was worthy
of the marriage torch, and told a shining lie
to her lying father, a maid whose name
    will live to all time.

'Rise!' she said to her young husband,
'Rise! Or you will receive a long sleep
from a hand you do not fear. Escape
    from my father and cruel sisters.   40

They are like pitiless she-lions, each tearing the flesh
of a young calf. I am not as they are.
I shall not strike you nor trap you
    behind locked doors.

Let my father heap cruel chains upon me
for taking pity on a defenceless husband.
Let him send me on his ships
    to Numidia's distant fields.

You go wherever your feet or the winds may take you,
while night and Venus grant their favour. Go   50
with good omen, and carve a lament for me
    on your tomb.'

XII

Miserarum est

Pity poor girls who cannot play love's game or wash
their ills away with a sweet wine without being half dead
        with fear of a lashing from an uncle's tongue.

The winged son of Cytherea steals your wool basket, Neobule,
the shining beauty of Hebrus of Lipara takes away your zeal
        for the work of Minerva

when he washes his shoulders glistening with oil
in Tiber's waves, a better horseman than Bellerophon,
            undefeated
        through slowness of fist or foot,

skilful, too, at spearing stags as they run over open ground
when the herd is in flight, and swift to face the boar   11
    lurking deep in the thicket.

XIII

O fons Bandusiae

O fountain of Bandusia, brighter than glass,
well do you deserve an offering of sweet wine
    and flowers, and tomorrow you will receive a kid
        with new horns bulging on his brow,

marking him out for love and war—
to no avail, since he will stain your cold stream
    with his red blood, this offspring
        of the amorous flock.

The cruel hour of the blazing Dog-star
cannot touch you. You give delicious   10
    coldness to oxen weary of the plough
        and the straggling flock.

You too will become a famous fountain
as I sing of the holm-oak
    above your cave in the rock
        where your waters leap down chattering.

XIV

Herculis ritu

You have just heard, O People of Rome, that Caesar
has sought the laurel whose cost is death,
    but now, like Hercules, he returns victorious from Spain
        to the gods of his home.

Let the wife of the great leader, rejoicing in the husband
who is her all-in-all, come forth worshipping

the just gods, his sister with her, and,
  adorned in the ribbons of suppliants,

the mothers of maidens and of young men
whose lives have just been saved. And you, boys 10
and girls who have not known a husband, beware
  of ill-omened words.

This holy day will truly drive away
all my black cares: I shall have no fear
of war or violent death while Caesar
  is master of the world.

Go, boy, and bring me fragrant oils, and garlands,
and a cask of wine that remembers the Marsian War,
if there is a jar anywhere that escaped
  the wandering Spartacus. 20

And tell the clear-voiced Neaera to waste no time
but put the myrrh on her hair and tie it up.
If the troublesome slave at her door makes any difficulty,
  just come away.

Greying hair mellows the spirit
that once relished disputes and violent quarrels;
I wouldn't have stood for this in the heat of my youth
  when Plancus was consul.

XV

Uxor pauperis Ibyci

Chloris, wife of impoverished Ibycus,
put an end to your naughtiness and
    your notorious struggle against the years.
The time is ripe for your funeral and here you are

    playing games with the girls,
casting a cloud over the shining stars.
    If it suits Pholoe, that does not mean
it suits you. Your daughter is the one who should

be storming young men's houses
clashing her tambourine like a Maenad.   10
    It's the love of Nothus
that makes her skip like a randy roe-deer.

Your place is with the famous wool
shorn round Luceria, not with lyres nor
    the crimson flower of the rose nor casks
drained to the dregs—you are an old woman.

XVI

Inclusam Danaen

Danaë, shut up behind stout doors in her tower
of bronze, and protected by fierce, unsleeping watchdogs
would have been fortified well enough
    against adulterers by night

if Jupiter and Venus had not laughed
at her frightened guard Acrisius—access
to the maiden's hiding place would be safe and easy
    if the god turned into the fee.

Gold loves to slip through sentries
and breaks down stone walls more effectively   10
than a flash of lightning. Bribery brought down
    the house of the augur of Argos

and overwhelmed it in disaster. The hero of Macedon
split the gates of cities and undermined
rival kings by means of gifts. Gifts put the noose
    on savage sea captains.

As money accumulates, anxiety and greed for more
come with it. I have refused to lift up my head
for all to see, and this is right,
    Maecenas, glory of the Knights.   20

The more a man denies himself, the more
he will receive from the gods. Naked, I go to join

the camp of those who desire nothing, and long
    to desert the ranks of the rich.

I am the master of a holding men despise, and prouder
than if I were said to be hiding away in my granaries
all the crops produced by the ploughs of hard-working Apulians,
    a pauper in the lap of wealth.

A stream of pure water, a few acres of woodland,
and a sure harvest, make me more blest by fortune   30
than the governor of grain-bearing Africa in all his glory—
    did he but know it.

Calabrian bees bring me no honey, for me
Bacchus does not languish in Laestrygonian cask,
and fat fleeces are not swelling
    in Gallic pastures,

but I suffer none of the pains of poverty,
and if I wanted more, you would not refuse it.
It is better for me to expand my little income
    by contracting my desires   40

than by joining the kingdom of Alyattes to the plains
of Mygdon of Phrygia. For those who ask much,
much is wanting. A man is doing well
    if God, with a thrifty hand, gives him enough.

XVII

Aeli vetusto

Aelius, distinguished descendant of old Lamus—
since they say that the early Lamias and the stock
    of their descendants through all recorded years
        took their name from him

and trace their origins to that founder king,
who is said to have been the first to have ruled
    the city of Formiae and the River Liris
        which floods Marica's shores,

the ruler of a broad domain—tomorrow a storm
will come down from the east   10
    and strew the wood with leaves and the shore
      with useless seaweed, unless the old crow

is a false prophet. Gather dry wood
while you may. Tomorrow you will tend
    your Genius with neat wine and a two–month–old pig,
      your slaves at ease about you.

XVIII

Faune, Nympharum

Faunus, who love the nymphs and make them run,
go gently through my land and the sunny countryside,
be kind and pass by without hurting
    the young of my flocks,

if I sacrifice a tender kidling when the year comes round,
if wine in abundance does not fail the mixing-bowl,
the crony of Venus, and the old altar
    smokes with a rich odour.

When the Nones of December come round,
the whole flock grazes on the grassy plain;   10
the country people make holiday in the meadows,
    oxen and all;

the wolf ambles among the fearless lambs;
the wood spreads its rustic foliage for you;
the ditcher's foot delights to thump in triple time
    the earth he so detests.

XIX

Quantum distet

How many years separate Inachus
from Codrus, who was not afraid to die for his country—

you tell us all about that and about the family tree
of Aeacus and wars fought beneath the walls of holy Troy,

but what we would pay for a jar
of Chian wine, who is to temper the water with fire,
whose house it is to be, and when I can escape
this Paelignian cold—not a word from you about that.

Give us wine right away for the new moon,
wine for the midnight, wine, boy, for the augur   10
Murena. With three or nine ladles
mix the cups and make sure they are full.

The poet struck by the thunderbolt,
lover of the uneven-numbered Muses, will demand
ladles three times three. More than three
the Grace with her naked sisters forbids

for fear of brawling.
Now is a time for madness. Why are the Berecyntian
horns not blowing?
Why is the pipe hanging there beside the silent lyre?   20

I hate stingy hands.
Strew the roses. Jealous Lycus must hear
the furious din. So must Lycus' lady,
our neighbour ill-yoked to an old man.

You, Telephus, with your sleek, thick hair,
you, Telephus, shining like the Evening Star in a cloudless sky,
are desired by young Rhode.
I am roasting in the slow heat of my love for Glycera.

XX

Non vides quanto

Don't you see, Pyrrhus, how dangerous it is
to steal the cubs from a Gaetulian lioness?
The robber will soon lose his courage
and run from deadly combat

as she cuts through the ranks of young warriors standing
in her way, to claim back her Nearchus—
a great tussle that will be to see which of you wins
    the richer booty.

Meanwhile, as you draw your swift arrows
from the quiver and she sharpens her fearsome teeth,   10
the arbiter of battle has set his naked foot
    on the palm of victory,

so they say, and in the gentle wind is cooling
his shoulders caressed by fragrant hair.
Like Nireus he is, or the boy once snatched
    from well-watered Ida.

XXI

O nata mecum

Born with me in the consulship of Manlius,
whether you bring complaints or jollity
    or brawls and lunatic loves,
        or easy sleep, O holy wine-jar,

under whatever name you preserve the choice Massic,
come down, you who deserve to be moved
    on a festal day. Corvinus is ordering me
        to bring out mellower wines.

Though steeped in Socratic dialogues,
he will not be so austere as to neglect you.   10
    Even old Cato's virtue, so they say,
        was warmed by unwatered wine.

You put natures at other times unbending
on a gentle rack; with your cheerful god Lyaeus
    you reveal the cares of the wise
        and their secret counsels;

you give hope back to anxious minds
and put horns on the poor man. After you

he does not tremble at the angry crowns
  of kings or soldiers' swords.   20

Bacchus, and Venus, if she comes in joy,
the Graces slow to untie the knot,
  and the living lamps will prolong you
    while Phoebus returning puts the stars to flight.

XXII

Montium custos

Guardian of mountains and woods, Virgin
who hear, when called three times by girls
in labour, and save them from death,
  three-formed goddess:

yours be the pine tree leaning over my villa
and at each year's end I will gladly give it
the blood of a young boar practising
  his sideways thrust.

XXIII

Caelo supinas

If when the moon is being born you lift your hands
upturned towards the sky, rustic Phidyle,
  if you placate the Lares with incense,
    this year's grain, and a greedy pig,

your vine will be fertile and not feel the wind
which brings disease from Africa, nor will your crop know
  the blight of mildew nor your lovely suckling beasts
    a time of danger when the year bears its fruit.

The sacrificial victim feeding
on snowy Algidus among oak and ilex   10
  or fattening in the Alban grasslands,
    will stain the axes of priests

with blood from its neck. There is no call for you
to ply your little gods with great killings
   of yearlings. Just crown them
      with rosemary or brittle sprigs of myrtle.

If your empty hand touches the altar, it is
more persuasive for offering no costly victim,
   and appeases angry Penates
      with consecrated grain and crackling salt.

XXIV

Intactis opulentior

   Though your riches surpassed
the untouched treasures of Arabia and all the wealth of India,
      though your building rubble
filled the Apulian and Tyrrhenian seas,

      if grim Necessity drives
her adamantine nail into your head,
      you will not free yourself
from fear or from the snares of death.

      The Scythians on their steppes
live better lives, carrying their nomadic homes   10
      in carts after their fashion;
the stern Getae too, whose unmeasured acres

      freely bear fruit and grain—
one year's cultivation is enough for them
      and on these same terms
their successor relieves them when a labour is over.

      There, the stepmother is gentle and kind
to her husband's motherless children, and the wife
      with a dowry does not lord it over
her husband or take a brilliant lover.   20

      The bride's rich dowry from her parents
is her virtue, a committed chastity

and fear of other men. Infidelity
is a sin against the gods. Its price is death.

Surely, if any man shall wish to put an end
to impious slaughter and the madness of civil strife,
     if he shall wish his statues
to be inscribed 'Father of Cities', let him have courage

     to rein back our wild licence, and so win fame
with posterity. With what meanness of spirit   30
     do we envy unblemished virtue,
yet long for it when it is removed from our sight!

     Why moan and grumble
and still fail to punish vice by cutting it away?
     Laws are useless without virtue.
What do they achieve, if nothing deters the merchant,

     not lands walled in by burning heat
nor regions lying flank to flank with Boreas,
     nor snow hardened on the earth;
if clever sailors master stormy seas,   40

     and if the supreme disgrace of poverty
makes men do and suffer anything,
     and desert the steep path of virtue?
If we truly feel remorse for our crimes,

     let us send our marble and jewels
and useless gold, the very stuff of vice,
     up to the Capitol,
urged on by the cries of eager crowds,

     or throw them into the nearest sea.
The early lessons of depraved desire must be   50
     erased from minds
that have been too tender and must now be moulded

     by harsher studies.
The free young Roman is not trained
     to stay on a horse.
He is afraid of hunting. His skill is rather in playing

with a Greek hoop, if you please,
or breaking the law by throwing dice,
    while his father gives his word
and breaks it, cheating his partner and the guest   60

of his house, to push money with all speed
towards his worthless heir. True, ill-gotten wealth
    accrues. Yet what he has
is never enough. More is always needed.

XXV

Quo me, Bacche, rapis

Where are you rushing me, Bacchus?
I am full of you. Into what woods or caverns do you drive me
    so swiftly with a mind not my own?
In what caves shall I be heard practising to set

    the deathless glory of great Caesar
among the stars and in the council of Jupiter?
    Grant that I may speak what is great and new,
unspoken till now by other lips. On mountain ridges

    the unsleeping Bacchant looks out
amazed over the Hebrus, over Thrace white   10
    with snow, and Rhodope
trodden by barbarian feet, just as I delight to gaze

    in wonderment at lonely woods
and river banks. O ruler of Naiads
    and of Bacchants whose mighty hands
pull down tall ash trees, let me say nothing

    small or in a humble tone,
nothing mortal. Sweet is the danger, Lenaeus,
    in following the god, wreathing
my forehead with the green tendrils of the vine.   20

XXVI

Vixi puellis nuper

Till now I have lived my life without complaints
from girls, and campaigned with my share of honours.
    Now my armour and my lyre—its wars are over—
        will hang on this wall

which guards the left side of Venus
of the sea. Here, over here, lay down my bright torches,
    the crowbars, and the bows that threatened
        opposing doors.

O goddess, who rule the blessed isle of Cyprus,
and Memphis never touched by Sithonian snow,   10
    lift high your whip, O Queen, and flick
        disdainful Chloe, just once.

XXVII

Impios parrae

Let evil omens see the impious on their way—
let the owl keep hooting, let a pregnant bitch
or grey wolf or vixen that has whelped come running down
    from the Lanuvian fields,

and may a snake break their journey after it has started,
darting across their path like an arrow, and terrifying
the ponies: I am an augur who can see the future
    and tell it to those for whom I fear.

My prayer shall rouse from the rising sun
the prophetic raven that foresees   10
the coming of rain, before it can fly back
    to the standing swamps.

May you be fortunate, Galatea—you will find it possible—
wherever you go, and may you always remember me.
May a magpie on the left not prevent your going
    nor a stray woodpecker.

But you see the wild, swift plunge
of Orion as he sets and I know well what mischief
the black gulf of the Adriatic can do
    and the clear wind of Iapyx.   20

May the wives and children of our enemies feel
the unseen movement of the South Wind as he rises,
the dark sea's roar, and the shore
    trembling under the lash,

like Europa, trusting her body to the bull
that betrayed her. Bold as she was she paled
in mid-ocean at the treachery of a sea
    teeming with monsters.

A little time before she was in a meadow gathering flowers
to plait a garland she had vowed to the nymphs,   30
but now in the glimmering night she saw nothing
    but stars and waves.

As soon as she came to land on mighty Crete
with its hundred cities, she cried 'O father,
I have forfeited the name of daughter. Duty
    was overcome by madness.

To think of what I left, and of what I now come to!
One death is not enough for a guilty woman. Am I awake,
deploring a crime I have committed?
    Or am I innocent,   40

mocked by an empty vision escaping
from the Gate of Ivory? Why did I cross
the wide sea waves and not stay
    to pick fresh flowers?

Now, if in my anger I had that vile bullock here,
I would do my best to rend him with a sword
and break the horns of the monster I loved
    so much so recently.

Shameless I abandoned the gods of my fathers.
Shameless I make the god of the Underworld wait for me.
Oh! I beg whatever god hears this that I should wander   51
    naked among lions.

Before my pretty cheeks are sunken and unsightly,
before the juice dies in the tender victim,
I want my body to feed the tigers
    while I am still beautiful.

"Worthless Europa!" urges my father far away,
"Why do you hesitate to die? You can hang yourself
from this ash tree in the girdle that has conveniently
    gone with you, and break your neck.   60

Or if you fancy cliffs and rocks, they are sharp and can kill—
go trust the storm wind, unless, being of royal blood,
you would prefer to be a drudge, plucking a daily darg
    of wool from the distaff,

the slave of a barbarian woman and
her husband's concubine."' As she lamented, Venus,
with a sly smile, and Cupid, his bowstring loosened,
    were standing by.

When in due course the goddess had had her fun,
'Curb your anger,' she said, 'and cool your ill-temper   70
when the bull you detest gives you
    his horns to rend.

You do not know that you are the wife
of almighty Jupiter. No more sobbing. You must learn
to endure your great good fortune. Half of the world
    will bear your name.'

XXVIII

Festo quid potius die

    What better thing could I do
on the day of Neptune's festival? Into action, Lyde,
    bring out the Caecuban I laid down,
and mount an assault on the fortress of wisdom.

    You see the sun is past the vertical.
The day is in full flight and you are taking your time

as though it were standing fast. Bring down
instantly that sluggish amphora of consul Bibulus.

We shall take turns and sing
of Neptune and the sea-green hair of the Nereids.   10
     In reply you will sing
to your curved lyre of Latona and the darts of swift Cynthia,

     and the last song will be of the goddess
who rules over Cnidos and the gleaming Cyclades, and visits
     Paphos in her swan-drawn chariot.
Night too will receive a well-deserved tribute in a sad lament.

XXIX

Tyrrhena regum progenies

Offspring of Etruscan kings, for you
a jar of mellow wine never yet disturbed,
     and roses in bloom, Maecenas,
          and balsam pressed for your hair

have long been waiting. Tear yourself free. No more delay.
Do not for ever contemplate watery Tibur
     and the sloping fields of Aefulae and
          the ridges of Telegonus the parricide.

Abandon your fastidiousness and luxury
and your huge pile whose neighbours are the soaring clouds.
     Stop admiring the splendour of Rome,   11
          its smoke, its wealth, its noise.

Variety has often brought delight to the rich,
and wholesome suppers under the little gods
     of a poor man's home—no tapestries, no purples—
          have often smoothed a worried brow.

The bright father of Andromeda is already showing
his hidden fire. Procyon is already raging
     and rabid Leo's star,
          as the sun brings back the days of drought.   20

The weary shepherd with his drowsy flock
is already making for the shade, the river,
    and the thickets of shaggy Silvanus.
        Silent the riverbank with no stray breath of wind.

You are worrying what constitution would best suit the state.
In your anxiety for the city you are afraid of the plots
    of the Chinese, of Cyrus's Bactrian kingdom,
        of the feuding peoples on the Don.

God foresees all future time and hides
what is to come in mist and darkness.   30
    He smiles if mortals fret
        too much. Make sure you deal calmly

with what is here. Everything else
flows by like a river, now gliding peacefully
    in mid-channel down to the Tuscan sea,
        now rolling down uprooted trees

and eroded rocks, cattle, and houses
all together with a great roaring of mountains
    and forest along its banks
        as the wild spate whips up   40

its peaceful flow. A man will be happy and in control
of his life if he can say at each day's end,
    'I have lived'. Tomorrow Father Jupiter
        can fill the sky with dark cloud

or cloudless sunlight, but he will not
annul what is behind us, nor
    will he remake or cancel
        what the flying hour has brought.

Fortune enjoys her cruel business and
persists in playing her proud game,   50
    transferring her fickle honours,
        favouring now me, now another.

I praise her while she stays. If she shakes out
her swift wings, I return what she gave, wrap myself

in my virtue, and look for honest Poverty,
   the bride that brings no dowry.

It is not my way, if the mast groans
in African gales, to take to pleading and praying
  and bargaining with the gods to keep
    my Tyrian and Cyprian cargo   60

from enriching the greedy sea.
When that time comes, the breeze and Pollux
  and his twin shall carry me safe in my two-oared dinghy
    through the Aegean storms.

XXX

Exegi monumentum

I have built a monument more lasting than bronze
and set higher than the pyramids of kings.
It cannot be destroyed by gnawing rain
or wild north wind, by the procession

of unnumbered years or by the flight of time.
I shall not wholly die. A great part of me
will escape Libitina. My fame will grow,
ever-renewed in time to come, as long as

the priest climbs the Capitol with the silent Virgin.
I shall be spoken of where fierce Aufidus thunders   10
and where Daunus, poor in water,
rules the country people. From humble beginnings

I was able to be the first to bring Aeolian song
to Italian measures. Take the proud honour
well-deserved, Melpomene, and be pleased
to circle my hair with the laurel of Delphi.

SECULAR HYMN

Phoebe silvarumque

Phoebus, and Diana, queen of forests,
shining glory of the sky, always worshipped
and always to be worshipped, grant our prayers
　　at this holy time

when the Sibylline verses have bidden
chaste and chosen boys and maidens
to sing a hymn to the gods who have loved
　　the seven hills.

Life-giving Sun, who with your gleaming chariot
display and then conceal the day, born for ever new　　10
and for ever the same, nothing can you see greater
　　than the city of Rome.

Ilithyia, who in season duly and gently open
the way to childbearing, protect all mothers,
whether your wish is to be called Lucina,
　　or Genitalis.

O goddess, bring the young to light, and prosper
the decrees of the Fathers which govern
the joining of man and woman, and ordain a law of marriage
　　rich in offspring,　　20

and may each fixed cycle of a hundred years and ten
bring back our hymns and games
crowded into three bright days
　　and three glad nights.

And you Parcae, ever singers of the truth, fulfil
what has been spoken—may the immovable boundary stone
of Fate preserve it—and join to our past greatness
　　a great destiny in the future.

Let Earth be rich in crops and cattle
and offer Ceres a wheat-ear crown,   30
and may Jupiter's wholesome showers and breezes
    nourish the young.

Sheathe your arrows, Apollo. Be mild and peaceful,
and listen to the boys praying.
Two-horned queen of the stars, O moon,
    listen to the girls.

O you gods, since Rome is your work, since through you
Trojan troops once reached the Etruscan shore, that small band
commanded to change its city and household gods
    and find safety in flight,   40

when the chaste Aeneas, who outlived his fatherland,
and carved a free path for his people,
unscathed through the burning city, to give them
    more than they had lost—

O you gods, grant good character to our young,
and peace and quiet to the old, and to the race of Romulus
prosperity, posterity,
    and every glory,

and whatever the noble blood of Anchises and Venus
prays for with offerings of white oxen,   50
let Rome receive, first in war, but merciful
    to a fallen enemy.

By land and sea the Mede now fears
Rome's mighty hands and the Alban axes,
Proud Scythians and Indians have just now come
    to crave audience.

There is Trust now, and Peace, Honour and Chastity;
ancient Virtue, long neglected,
dares to return, and rich Abundance is amongst us
    with full horn.   60

But Phoebus, the god of augury, in all his beauty
with his golden bow, whom the nine Muses love,
who relieves weary limbs
    with his healing arts—

when he sees the altars on the Palatine and approves,
for another cycle of the years he then preserves
the Roman state and the blessings of Latium
    and leads us on to ever greater glories.

And Diana, ruler of Algidus and Aventine,
heeds the prayers of the Fifteen   70
and lends a loving ear
    to children's vows.

And I report a good and certain hope
that Jupiter and all the gods assent to this,
I, who am the chorus taught to sing the praises
    of Phoebus and Diana.

ODES, BOOK IV

I

Intermissa, Venus

Back to war, Venus, after all
these years? Spare me, spare me, I beg you.
    I'm not the man I was
in good Cinara's reign. Cruel mother

    of the sweet Cupids, stop
driving a long-since-hardened fifty-year-old
    with your soft commands. Away with you!
Go and answer the charming prayers of young men.

    If you are looking for a proper liver
to roast, it's time for you to go carousing,   10
    winged by your lustrous swans,
to the home of Paulus Maximus.

    He is noble, comely,
not slow to speak for those accused and in distress,
    a lad with all the arts,
who will carry far and wide the standards of your wars,

    and when he has prevailed
over his rival and laughed at his lavish gifts,
    he will set you up in marble
among the Alban lakes under a beam of citrus wood.   20

    There will your nostrils breathe
clouds of incense and you will take delight
    in mingled notes of lyre
and Berecyntian horn, and reed-pipes too.

    There twice a day will boys
and tender maidens praise your godhead,
    beating the earth
with shinning feet in triple Salian time.

As for me, I no longer take pleasure in woman
or boy, nor in the fond hope that my love might still   30
    be returned, nor in drinking bouts,
not in binding my brow with fresh flowers.

But why, Ligurinus, o why,
is that tear trickling down my cheek?
    Why does my glib tongue
fall shamefully silent as I speak?

At night in my dreams sometimes I catch
and hold you, sometimes I pursue you as you run
    over the grass of the Campus Martius
or swim, so hard of heart, the rolling waves.   40

II

Pindarum quisquis

All those, Iullus, who aim to rival Pindar,
are struggling on feathers waxed by the art
of Daedalus, and will give their names
    to the glassy sea.

Like a rain-fed river running down
from the mountains and bursting its banks—
seething, immeasurable, deep-mouthed,
    Pindar races along in spate,

winning the laurel of Apollo as he rolls
new words down the bold current   10
of his dithyrambs, rushing along in rhythms
    that know no law,

or as he sings of gods or kings, blood-line
of gods, by whom the Centaurs
fell in just death, by whom fell
    the fierce Chimaera's fires,

or as he tells of boxer or of charioteer,
heavenly ones brought home by the palm

of victory from Elis, and gives a prize
  worth a hundred statues,   20

or as he laments the young man torn
from his weeping bride, and raises to the stars
his golden valour, his virtues, his spirit,
  to cheat black Orcus.

Many a breeze lifts the swan of Dirce
whenever he soars into the tracts of cloud;
as for me, to the style and measure
  of the Matine bee,

all round the well-watered woods and river banks
of Tibur I work busily, sipping   30
the harvest of sweet thyme and shaping
  my laborious poems.

You, Iullus, will be the poet to sing to a mightier
plectrum of Caesar dragging the fierce Sugambri
up the Sacred Hill, with the garland of glory
  justly on his forehead.

A greater blessing than Caesar, the fates and kindly gods
have never given to the earth and never will give
though Time should return
  to the Age of Gold.   40

You will be the poet to sing of the days of joy,
of a whole city at play, and a Forum without lawsuits,
all celebrating the return of Augustus
  in answer to our prayers.

Then, if my words deserve a hearing, the best
of my voice will add its part, and I shall rejoice
at Caesar's return, crying, 'we sing your praises,
  Heavenly Sun,'

and as you, O god of Triumph, go in procession,
the whole city will shout your name 'Io Triumphe!'   50
and shout again 'Io Triumphe!' and we shall send up incense
  to the kindly gods.

Ten cows, Iullus, and ten bulls will discharge your dues;
for mine a tender calf will be enough, just taken
from its mother and growing to maturity in rich pasture,
    to pay my vow,

copying with the white mark
on its forehead the curved fires
of the third rising of the moon,
    otherwise pure brown.   60

III

Quem tu, Melpomene

    The man you have once looked upon
at his birth, Melpomene, with kindly eye—
      no toil at the Isthmus
will make him a famous boxer, no tireless horse

    will take him to victory
in a Greek chariot, nor will feats of war
      make a general of him parading on the Capitol
and crowned with Delian leaves

    for crushing the swelling threats of kings;
but the waters which flow past fertile Tibur   10
      and thick tresses of forest foliage
will make him famous for Aeolian song.

    The young of Rome, chief of cities,
see fit to place me among the choirs of the bards
      they love, and envy's tooth
no longer bites so keenly. O goddess

    of Pieria, who temper
the sweet noise of the golden shell of the lyre,
      o goddess, who if you wished
could grant to dumb fish the song of the swan,   20

this is all your gift,
that people as they pass point to me
    as the player of the Roman lyre.
That I breathe, and give pleasure, if I give pleasure, is due to you.

IV

Qualem ministrum

Like the winged lightning-bearer to whom the king
of the gods has entrusted the kingdom of the birds of the air
    —Jupiter tested him and found him true
        in the capture of golden-haired Ganymede—

his maturing age and the vigour he inherits
thrust him from the nest long since, before he knew
    what lay before him, and then the winds of spring,
        clearing away the clouds, taught him his new tasks,

nervous as he was; but soon his impetus sent him
swooping down upon the sheepfolds, and now   10
    his love of feasting and battle have driven him
        to attack the writhing serpent;

or like the lion whelp just driven from the rich milk
of his tawny mother, when the roe-deer intent on grazing
    rich pastures sees him suddenly and dies
        in jaws till then unblooded—

so did the Vindelici see Drusus waging war
at the foot of the Raetian Alps. Whence comes
    their ancient practice of arming
        their right hands with Amazonian axes   20

I have forborne to ask, for it is not right
to know all things, but their cohorts,
    for long ages victorious far and wide,
        were crushed by a young man's wisdom,

and learned what inborn mind and character
could do, if duly trained in a home blest

by the gods, and what the fatherly spirit of Augustus
    could achieve for the young Nerones.

The brave are born from the brave and good.
In cattle, in horses, you find the virtues   30
    of the sires. The fierce eagle does not hatch
        the timorous dove,

yet training advances inborn powers,
and sound practice strengthens the spirit in the breast.
    When character fails, the faults
        are a disgrace to the breeding.

Consider, O city of Rome, what you owe to the Nerones—
witness the river Metaurus, the crushing
    of Hasdrubal, and that bright day
        when darkness was driven from Latium,   40

the first to smile in kindness and glory
since the African rode through the cities of Italy
    like flame through a pine forest
        or East wind over the Sicilian waves.

Since then the youth of Rome have grown in strength
by constant labour and achievement, the gods
    have stood erect in shrines once ravaged
        by that impious rabble from Carthage,

and perfidious Hannibal has said at last:
'We are deer, the helpless prey of ravenous wolves,   50
    and the richest triumph we can hope for
        is to cheat them and escape.

The race which rose in courage from the ashes
of Troy and was tossed on Tuscan seas,
    has carried all the way to the cities of Italy
        its sacraments, its sons, and its aged fathers.

Like a holm-oak stripped by cruel double axes
on the fertile dark-leaved slopes of Algidus,
    it suffers loss and death, but gathers
        power and life from the very steel.   60

It matches the Hydra, which gained strength
from every cut and made Hercules despair of victory,
    nor did the Colchians nor Echion's Thebes
        produce a greater miracle.

Sink them in the deep; they will rise more glorious.
Wrestle with them; to loud applause they will throw
    the unbeaten champion and fight battles
        to be the talk of their wives.

To Carthage I shall not now be sending
proud messages. Fallen, fallen, are all the hopes   70
    and all the fortune of our people
        now that Hasdrubal is dead.

No task is too great for the hands of the Claudians.
Jupiter defends them by his kindly favour,
    and wisdom and care speed them
        through the cutting blades of war.'

V

Divis orte bonis

Offspring of the good gods and best guardian
of the race of Romulus, too long have you been absent.
You promised the sacred council of the Fathers
    a swift return, so return.

Give back your radiance, good leader, to your homeland.
When your face shines like springtime
on your people, the day passes more joyfully
    and the sun is brighter.

As a mother calls with vows and prayers and the taking
of omens, upon her young son detained across   10
the Carpathian sea by the jealous blasts of the South wind,
    as he waits till the sailing year is over,

far from the home he loves, and she never
takes her eyes from the curve of the shore,

so does your faithful homeland, stricken with longing,
     look for its Caesar.

The ox now wanders the fields in perfect safety.
The fields are fed by Ceres and the kindly god of Plenty.
Sailors fly across the peaceful sea.
     Truth shrinks from the shame of untruth.   20

The chaste home is unsullied by debauchery.
Law written and unwritten has subdued wickedness.
Mothers are praised for bearing true sons of their fathers.
     The presence of punishment prevents sin.

Who could tremble at the Parthian? At the chilly Scythian?
At the shaggy brood that Germany produces,
while Caesar is safe? Who could think of war
     with the savages of Spain?

Every man weds the vine to the maiden tree
and sees the sun go down on his own hills,   30
then goes cheerily home to his wine and invites you,
     Caesar, as a god, to the second course.

To you he offers libation with many prayers and for you
he pours neat wine from the chalice, joining
your divine majesty to his household gods, as Greece
     remembers Castor and great Hercules.

'Good leader, grant, we pray, long days
of ease to Hesperia,' so we say, dry
at dawn when the day is new, and not so dry
     when the sun is under the sea.   40

VI

Dive, quem proles

God, who punish the boastful tongue, as the children
of Niobe discovered, god, whom the ravisher Tityos
came to know, and Phthian Achilles,
   so nearly the conqueror of lofty Troy,

greatest warrior of them all, but no match for you
although he was the son of Thetis, goddess of the sea,
and shook the towers of Dardanus, fearsome
 in battle with his spear—

he fell like a pine tree hacked by the biting edge
of steel or a cypress struck by the east wind,   10
and lay his great length, with his head
 in the dust of Troy;

he was not the man to shut himself in the wooden horse,
that false offering to Minerva, or lure the Trojans
into foolish celebrations and surprise the court of Priam
 dancing with delight,

but would have taken his enemies in open combat
and shown no mercy, shame! shame! burning
infant children in Achaean fires, and even
 the baby hiding in the womb,   20

if the Father of the Gods had not been swayed
by your words and the words of his beloved Venus
to allow Aeneas to lay out his walls
 under better auspices—

Phoebus, teacher of Thalia's shrill lyre,
who wash your hair in the waters of Xanthus,
preserve the glory of the Daunian Muse,
 O smooth-cheeked Agyieus.

Phoebus has given me the art, the very breath
of song. Phoebus has given me the name of poet. 30
Noblest of maidens and sons
 of the noblest fathers,

all in the care of the Delian goddess who with her bow
checks deer and lynxes as they run,
keep the beat of the Lesbian verse
 and follow my thumb,

singing with due care the praise of the son of Latona,
singing with due care of Noctiluca with her growing torch,
who prospers the crops and hurries on
 the swiftly rolling months.   40

In time to come when you are a Roman wife, you will say,
'When the Secular Festival brought back its lights,
I performed the hymn which so pleased the gods,
    and was taught the music of the poet Horace.'

VII

Diffugere nives

The snow has fled, grass is now coming back to the fields
    and leaves to the trees,
the earth is making its change. Rivers are going down
    and flowing between their banks.

A naked Grace dares to lead the dance of her two sisters
    and the Nymphs.
Do not hope for immortality—the year gives warning and the
        hour
    that hurries along the life-giving day.

The cold melts in the Zephyrs, Summer tramples on the heels
    of Spring, and will die the moment   10
Autumn laden with fruit pours out her crops, and soon
    sluggish Winter comes running back.

Swift moons make good their losses in the sky,
    but when we go down to be
with pious Aeneas, wealthy Tullus, and Ancus,
    we are dust and shadow.

Who knows if the gods above will add the hours of tomorrow
    to the total of today?
Whatever you give your own dear self will escape
    the greedy hands of your heir.   20

When you are dead and Minos has passed on you
    his splendid judgements,
not all your ancestry, Torquatus, nor eloquence, nor piety
    will bring you back.

Diana does not rescue her chaste Hippolytus
    from the darkness beneath the earth,

nor does Theseus have the strength to break the Lethean
    chains
      that bind his dear Pirithous.

VIII

Donarum pateras

I would gladly give proper gifts to my friends,
goblets and bronzes. I would give them tripods,
prizes won by Greek heroes, and you,
Censorinus, would not be receiving

the worst of them—if, that is, I had a rich collection
of works produced by Scopas in stone, or Parrhasius
in coloured liquids, skilled both of them
to represent both god and man.

But this is not my strength, and your tastes
and way of life do not require such luxuries.   10
It is song you love; and we can give you
song and put a price on the gift.

Not marble slabs incised with public records
bringing breath and life back to great leaders
after death, not Hannibal's swift flight
or his threats thrown back in his teeth,
[*not the burning of impious Carthage*]

—none of these confers such clear praise
on the man who bought the name of Africanus
by conquering Africa, as do the Muses of Calabria.   20
If paper does not speak about your achievements,

you will win no reward. What would Romulus be
if jealous silence blurred the merits
of that son of Ilia and Mars?
The courage and favour of mighty poets, their very tongues,

rescued Aeacus from the waves of the Styx and consecrated
a home for him in the Isles of the Blest. When a man

deserves praise, the Muse forbids him to die.
The Muse grants the sky. Through her does unwearying
     Hercules

share in Jupiter's banquets, as he so longed to do;   30
the bright stars Castor and Pollux
catch up shattered ships from the bottom of the sea;
[*with temples crowned with green sprigs of the vine*]
Bacchus leads prayers to fulfilment.

IX

Ne forte credas

Lest you should suppose they will perish—
these words written by one born by the far-sounding
    Aufidus, for setting to the lyre
        by arts not known before—

though Maeonian Homer sits in the seat of honour,
other Muses are not lost to sight, the Pindaric
    or the Cean, the menacing for Alcaeus,
        the grave for Stesichorus,

nor has time erased the cheerful poems
of Anacreon, and still there breathes   10
    the ardour of love entrusted to the lyre
        by the girl from Aeolia.

Helen of Sparta was not the only woman
to burn with desire for an adulterer's
    well-groomed hair and clothes spangled with gold,
        for kingly pomp and retinue.

Nor was Teucer the first to aim arrows
from a Cretan bow, and Troy was besieged
    more than once. Great Idomeneus and Sthenelus
        were not the only men to fight battles   20

worthy of the Muses, and Hector
and bold Deiphobus were not the first
   to suffer grievous wounds defending
     their children and their wives.

Many brave men have lived before Agamemnon,
but, unwept and unknown, they are all crushed
   under eternal night
     because they have no sacred poet.

Courage unseen differs little
from cowardice dead and buried. I will not leave you   30
   unsung, Lollius, in what I write,
     nor easily suffer all your great labours

to be gnawed away by envy and oblivion.
You have a mind wise in affairs,
   upright in prosperity
     and in times of doubt,

stern in punishing greed and fraud, holding aloof
from money whose lure nothing can resist,
   consul not for one year, but whenever,
     as a sound and incorruptible judge,   40

you put truth before expediency,
with head held high spurning the gifts of powerful men,
   and opening with your sword a triumphant
     path through the enemy cohorts.

The man who owns little could be called
truly blessed; even more truly
   is that title claimed by the man who uses
     wisely the gifts of the gods,

who endures the rigour of poverty
and fears disgrace worse than death.   50
   Not for him to be afraid to die
     for those he loves or for his homeland.

X

O crudelis adhuc

Still cruel and still enjoying the power
    that Venus gives,
when the feather you hope never to see appears
    in the plumage of your pride,

and the hair now floating round your shoulders
    is cut and lying on the ground,
and that complexion, which now beggars
    the crimson of the rose

has changed, Ligurinus,
    to bristles,   10
every time you look in the mirror and see you are not you,
    you will say 'Alas!

Why, when I was a boy, was I not minded
    as I am today?
or why, minded as I am, do I not once again
    have perfect cheeks?'

XI

Est mihi nonum

There is a cask full of Alban wine seeing out
its ninth year. There is celery in the garden,
Phyllis, for weaving garlands.
    There is a great wealth

of ivy for binding your hair to dazzle our eyes.
The house is smiling with silver, the altar, bound
with sacred green, longs to be spattered with blood
    from the sacrificial lamb,

the whole household is at the run, slave girls
and boys rushing back and forth,   10

tips of whirling flames
  throwing off sooty smoke.

But so that you may know what joys
you are called to, you are to celebrate the Ides,
the day which splits April, the month
  of Venus of the sea,

the day I rightly hold in honour and revere more almost
than the day of my own birth, because
from this dawn's light my Maecenas puts in order
  the years which flow to his account.   20

Young Telephus, whom you desire, is not for you.
A girl who is wealthy and eager for love,
has captured him and keeps him shackled
  in delicious fetters.

Scorched Phaethon deters all greedy hopes
and winged Pegasus, weighed down
by his earthly rider Bellerophon,
  provides a weighty example

to teach you to aim at what is proper for you,
to judge it a sin to hope for more than is allowed,   30
and to avoid a partner who is not your equal.
  Come then, last of my loves

—for after this I shall never warm to any other woman—
master these melodies to sing back to me
with your lovely voice. Black cares
  will be lessened by song.

XII

Iam veris comites

Now the friends of spring, the Thracian winds
that calm the sea, are driving on the sails,
ice has left the fields, and rivers have stopped roaring,
  no longer swollen with winter snow.

The unhappy swallow builds her nest, mourning
for Itys, and the undying shame brought on the house
of Cecrops by the barbarous lust of kings
    and by her cruel revenge.

In soft young grass the shepherds tend
plump sheep and sing songs to the reed pipe,   10
pleasuring the god who loves the flocks
    and dark hills of Arcadia.

The season has brought on thirst. But if you are longing,
Virgil, to drink the juice of Bacchus squeezed
from Calenian presses, you will pay for wine with nard,
    you client of the young nobility.

A tiny phial of nard will tempt out the cask
that lies in Sulpicius' cellars
with all its gifts of new hope and all its power
    to wash away the bitterness of care.   20

If you are eager for these joys, come quick
and bring your contribution. It is not my intention
to let you bathe in my cups scot free—
    this is no rich man's house.

But lay aside delay and thought of gain,
remember the black fires of death, and while you may
blend a little foolishness into your plans.
    Folly is delightful in its place.

XIII

Audivere, Lyce

The gods have listened, Lyce, the gods have listened
to my prayers; you're becoming an old woman
    and you still want to be thought beautiful,
        you still play about and you drink too much,

and sing in your cups in that wobbling voice of yours
to rouse the sluggish god of love, but he is out

> for the night, on duty on the lovely cheeks
> of a young Chian lyre-player.

That demanding god soars over dry oaks.
He flies away from you, your black teeth   10
> your wrinkles, and the snow
> in your hair. You are ugly.

Neither Coan purples nor precious stones
bring back the time
> buried in old calendars
> by the swiftly flying days.

Where has your charm gone? Where is your complexion?
Where is that lovely way of moving? What remains
> of the girl, who breathed the breath of love,
> who stole me from myself,   20

the girl I so loved after Cinara, and where is
that artful beauty of yours I knew so well? But the Fates,
> who did not give Cinara many years,
> were to keep you alive

as long as any ancient crow, to raise
a laugh among hot-blooded young men
> as they see your torch
> crumbling into ashes.

XIV

Quae cura patrum

What efforts by the Senate, what efforts by the citizens,
could immortalize your virtues, Augustus
> and pay you due honour in inscriptions
> and on commemorative days,

O greatest of princes wherever the sun
bathes habitable shores in light?
> Ignorant of Latin law, the Vindelici
> have just learned

what you could do in war. With your soldiers,
Drusus has repaid with interest the swift Breuni   10
    and the Genauni, a race that knew not peace,
      and cast down their citadels

perched on the tremendous Alps, and soon
the elder Nero fought a grim battle
    under your blest auspices and routed
      the mighty Raeti,

for all to see him deal destruction in the lists
of war and wear out the hearts of men who freely chose
    to dedicate themselves to death.
      Like the south wind   20

driving on the waves of the irresistible sea when the chorus
of Pleiads cleaves the clouds, tireless he was
    in harrying the enemy squadrons and riding
      his foaming horse through fire and flame.

So too rolls the bull river Aufidus
round Daunus' Apulian kingdom, preparing
    in his rage to loose fearsome flood
      upon the farmlands,

like Claudius, bursting the steel-clad barbarian lines,
victorious and unscathed in devastating onset,   30
    and strewing the ground as he harvested
      the enemy ranks from front to rear

while you gave the armies, you gave the counsel
and your own favouring gods. On the very day
    the port of Alexandria submitted
      and threw open its empty palace,

after years three times five, propitious Fortune
has again brought war to favourable issue and added
    the honour and glory we have prayed for
      to all the campaigns you have fought.   40

O present and potent guardian of Italy and of Rome
her mistress, the Cantabrian hitherto unsubdued
    and Mede and Indian now revere you,
      and Scythian famous in retreat.

Nile, too, adores, who hides the source of his waters,
Danube, the predatory Tigris, and the home
    of sea monsters, Oceanus,
        howling at the distant Britons,

while Gaul that fears not death, the harsh land
of Spain, and the Sugambri who delight   50
    in slaughter have laid down their weapons
        and venerate your name.

XV

Phoebus volentem

I was eager to sing of battles and defeated cities,
but Phoebus struck his lyre and forbade me
    to sail my little boat
        across the Tyrrhenian sea. Your Augustan age,

Caesar, has given rich crops back
to our fields, has brought the standards back to our Jupiter,
    tearing them from the proud door-posts
        of the Parthians, has cleared War

out of the Gate of Janus Quirinus and closed it, has forced
a bridle on Licence as it wandered off the straight path,   10
    has driven off our wickedness
        and summoned back the ancient arts

by which once grew the people of Latium and the might
of Italy, and by which the fame and majesty of empire
    were extended to the rising of the sun
        from his bed in the West.

While Caesar is guardian of the state, neither civil war
nor civil madness will drive away our peace,
    nor will anger beat out its swords
        and set city against unhappy city,   20

nor will those who drink the deep waters
of the Danube break the Julian edicts, nor will Getae,

nor Chinese, nor treacherous Persians,
   nor men born on the banks of the Don;

and on ordinary days as on holy days,
among the gifts of cheerful Bacchus, let us first
   with our children and our wives
     offer due prayers to the gods

and sing a song to the Lydian pipe in praise
of leaders who have shown the virtues   30
   of their fathers, in praise of Troy, Anchises,
     and the offspring of life-giving Venus.

EXPLANATORY NOTES

EPODES

I

It is the summer of 31 BC and Octavian (in line 3 called Caesar), facing the 500 ships of Antony and Cleopatra off the north-west coast of Greece, has summoned all Romans of consequence to Brindisi to support him. Maecenas, Horace's patron, has not included the poet in his entourage.

1   *Liburnians*: the translation has added the word 'light' to hint at the popular notion of the battle of Actium as the defeat of Antony's armada of huge galleons by Octavian's lighter, swifter ships modelled upon those sailed by Liburnian pirates in the north Adriatic.

28   The owner of wide estates could feed his stock in the valleys in the winter and have them driven up to the hills for summer pasture before the heat came with the Dog-star in July.

30   *Circe's son*: Telegonus, son of Circe, was the reputed founder of Tusculum, a favoured resort of wealthy Romans. For Circe see note on xvii. 17.

33   *Chremes*: a name commonly given to stingy old men in Roman comedy.

II

7   *Forum . . . lofty doors*: commercial, legal, political, and social business was transacted in the Forum. Imposing doorways were a mark of wealth and importance, and clients paying daily respects to patrons would be well aware of them.

20   *purple*: another mark of wealth and power.

21   *Priapus*: the god of gardens.

59   *Terminus*: the god of boundaries.

60   *snatched from the wolf*: no wastage here.

67   *Alfius*: the speaker who praised the countryman unencumbered by debt (4), turns out to be a moneylender. The Ides are on the thirteenth or fifteenth day of the month; the Kalends are the first.

III

7 *Canidia*: the witch of *Epodes* v and xvii. Horace may be mischievously playing with the fact that Publius Canidius Crassus was a loyal supporter of Antony and led his land forces at the battle of Actium. He was put to death by Octavian in 30 BC.

9–14 *Medea*: when Jason and the Argonauts came to Colchis on the eastern shore of the Black Sea to win the Golden Fleece, Jason had to yoke fire-breathing bulls. Horace pretends that garlic was the deterrent Medea prescribed against them. Jason took her back to Greece with him, but when he was about to marry Creusa, daughter of the king of Corinth, Medea gave her a poisoned dress which burned in contact with her skin. Medea then killed her own children by Jason, and escaped in a chariot drawn by winged serpents.

18 *Hercules*: Hercules killed the Centaur Nessus when he attempted to rape Hercules' wife Deianira. As he died Nessus gave her a shirt impregnated with fire, and told her that she should give it to Hercules if ever she doubted his love.

IV

Horace addresses the ex-slave in the first half of the poem. One passer-by speaks to another in the second.

3 *Spanish ropes*: the target of this lampoon had not only been a slave, he had also been a good-for-nothing slave, frequently flogged and chained. Ropes were made from esparto grass, of which large quantities were grown around Cartagena on the south-east tip of Spain.

11 *the triumvirs' lash*: the triumvirs were the commission of three responsible for prisons and for capital and corporal punishment. The crier had presumably to count the strokes.

16 *Otho's law*: the Roscian Law (57 BC) was passed in the tribunate of L. Roscius Otho. It reserved the first fourteen seats in the theatre for the Knights, the *equites*. No doubt Horace's enemy had amassed enough wealth by a military career not only to buy a prime vineyard in the Falernian country, but also to meet the Knights' property qualification (cf. i. 23–30), but the law seems also to have stipulated that no one who had been born a slave could become an *eques*.

18 *two-ton*: literally 'of heavy weight'. Of the thirty-three beaks of Antony's ships which Octavian/Augustus dedicated at Actium after the battle in 31 BC, the heaviest weighed two tons. The

reference to pirates suggests that this poem is set during the sea battles against Sextus Pompeius in 37–36 BC (Dio il. 1). It also suggests that the addressee had once been a pirate and a slave.

20   *admiral*: literally 'military tribune'. He would have been in command of soldiers fighting on shipboard.

V

A free Roman boy (see note on line 7) has been captured by a coven of witches including Canidia, Sagana, Veia, and Folia (lines 15, 25, 29, 41). As the poem begins they suddenly burst in and strip him naked. He appeals to them all at first, but in line 5 the second person is singular, and he is addressing their leader Canidia.

5–6 *honest childbirth*: for false claims see xvii. 50. Lucina (6) is the goddess of childbirth.

7   *the purple*: Roman boys wore the toga with a purple stripe, the *toga praetexta*.

12   *finery*: in addition to the *toga praetexta* Roman boys wore a gold pendant round the neck, the *bulla*.

21–4 *Iolcus . . . Hiberia . . . Colchian*: all famous for witchcraft and magic. Iolcus was in Thessaly, the port from which Jason sailed to capture the Golden Fleece. Hiberia, modern Georgia, was east of Colchis, home of Medea (see note on iii. 9–14). In 36 BC it was conquered by Canidius (see note on iii. 7).

41–3 *Ariminum . . . Neapolis*: now Rimini and Naples.

50–82 Canidia's speech opens with an address to goddesses, but at line 61 she realizes that her normal potions have failed to win back her aged lover despite the fact that she has given him magic unguents to put on (59). For Medea (61) see note on iii. 9–14. In 73 at last she reveals that the lover's name is Varus and addresses him, warning that she is going to make him drink a stronger potion, no doubt containing the ingredients described in line 37.

51   *Diana*: the triple goddess of the countryside, the moon, and the Underworld. In this last capacity she is often addressed as Hecate and invoked in magic rites.

57   *Subura*: a busy and disreputable district of Rome.

76   *Marsians*: a people of central Italy, famous for their sorcery.

86   *Thyestean*: Thyestes cursed his brother Atreus when Atreus served him a dish consisting of his own sons.

99   *the Esquiline*: the common graveyard of the poor (*Satires* I. viii, 10). Two other poems at least allude to witches on the Esquiline, *Satires*

I. iii, and *Epode* xvii. 58. Horace is surely playing with the fact that his patron Maecenas had bought up land on this hill and built a superb palace and gardens.

VI

It would be wrong to make heavy weather of this cheerful poem, but Horace seems to tell us that he is warning off some critic who has attacked an innocent victim. The critic is seen as a dog barking at passers-by from the safety of a farm. To bribe him into silence, the farmer throws out some scraps of food. In line 5 Horace compares himself to a hunting dog of formidable Greek breed but by lines 11–12 he has become a bull. In the couplet which follows he claims to be like Archilochus, who wooed Lycambes' daughter, was refused, and by his verse drove Lycambes to suicide; or like Hipponax, who had violent words for the sculptor Bupalo, whose statue of the poet displeased the sitter.

VII

The dramatic date of this poem may be after the piracy in 42–39 BC of Sextus Pompeius, who had taken Neptune (line 4) as his patron. In 39 BC Pompeius, Antony, and Octavian had signed the treaty of Puteoli, but early in 38 Pompeius and Octavian were preparing to resume fighting (lines 1–2). In 40 BC the Parthians had taken advantage of these civil wars to overrun Syria and Cilicia (line 10).

VIII

11–12 *effigies . . . triumphator*: wax effigies of ancestors were carried in procession at Roman funerals. The lady is so old that Horace looks at her and thinks of her funeral. The triumph was the highest public distinction.

15 *Stoic tracts*: the Stoics prided themselves on their virtue and austerity. This woman is therefore exposed as a hypocrite, as well as a blue-stocking and a fool.

IX

It seems that Horace and Maecenas are on board ship after the battle of Actium (line 27) and have just heard of the flight of Antony and Cleopatra.

3 *lofty home*: Horace is wistfully looking forward to returning to convivial pleasures in Maecenas' palace in Rome.

7 *Neptune's admiral*: Sextus Pompeius (see note on *Epode* vii) had been defeated at Naulochus in 36 BC.

13–16 *stakes . . . eunuchs . . . mosquito nets*: this satirizes the behaviour of Antony's troops at the court of Cleopatra and on campaign before the battle of Actium. Roman soldiers carried stakes for building palisades.

17 *Galli*: these are not Gauls here, but Galatians from Asia Minor who came over to Octavian's side just before the battle. Nevertheless, the thought of Galli singing the praises of Caesar would put a Roman reader in mind of other Galli and another Caesar, the Gauls whom Julius had conquered in the fifties BC.

19–20 *pulled to port*: this takes a simple view of a fiercely contested passage, suggesting that when Antony's fleet was sailing south down the coast of Greece it changed course and sailed eastwards to take refuge in harbour. The ships turn sharply to the left. The translator must use the word 'port' and this could set up a muddle with the Latin word *portus* in the next line, meaning 'harbour'. This translation attempts to solve the problem by naming the port, and by translating *portus* as 'the Ambracian Gulf'.

21–3 *Io Triumphe*: the cry of the spectators at a Roman triumph.

23 *Jugurtha*: king of Numidia in North Africa. Marius and Sulla were the great Roman generals engaged in the Jugurthine War which ended in 107 BC.

25 *Africanus*: Publius Scipio Africanus Minor was the Roman commander at the destruction of Carthage in 146 BC.

29–31 *Crete . . . Syrtes*: by this vivid touch Horace gives us an insight into the realities of sea battles, in which the position of the enemy is often a matter for speculation. Antony would naturally be making for Egypt, in which case Crete would be on his course. Alternatively, he might be trying to join his remaining legions near the Syrtes in Cyrenaica. Notus, strictly the south-west wind, would not make for an easy landfall in this coast line of shifting sand.

36 *seasickness*: Roman writings on wine are heavily concerned with its medicinal effects. Wine is said by Pliny to check vomiting (*Natural History* xxiii. 38), but Horace can scarcely be serious here. It sounds like a cheerful excuse.

38 *Lyaeus*: a title of Bacchus, god of wine, in Greek 'the Releaser'.

X

2   *Maevius*: Virgil attacks a poet of this name at *Eclogues* iii. 90.

10   *Orion*: the setting of Orion in November often comes in stormy weather.

14   *Ajax*: the virgin goddess Pallas Athena championed the Greeks at Troy, but destroyed Ajax, son of Oileus, on his homeward journey, in retribution for his rape of Cassandra, the Trojan priestess of Apollo.

24   *randy*: and therefore stinking, to make an offering appropriate to Maevius and an effective ring composition.

XI

This epode is unusual in that the even lines are longer than the odd. In *Epodes* xi–xvi the metres are mixtures of iambics and dactyls. Dactylic metres do not work in English so this translation continues to use iambics, except in xi and xii, which blend iambics with prose to give some sort of sample of the flavour of the original.

XII

11   *crocodile*: according to Pliny's *Natural History* xxviii. 108, the land crocodile likes to eat sweet-smelling flowers, and its intestines, being full of a fragrant juice called *crocodilea*, are much in demand, *inter alia* for clearing the complexion of blotches, freckles, pimples, and spots.

16   *Lesbia*: readers of Catullus would know that a Lesbia is a promiscuous woman. If she were still alive in 30 BC she would be in her mid-fifties.

XIII

4   *spry*: in Latin 'green'.

6   *my Torquatus*: dates, including the vintages of wine, were given by the names of the consuls of the year. The Torquati were a distinguished Roman family. Lucius Manlius Torquatus is called 'my Torquatus' because he was consul in 65 BC, the year in which Horace was born. Wine made from grapes pressed in that year would have been 35 years old when these poems were published.

9   *Cyllenian*: Mount Cyllene in Arcadia was the birthplace of Mercury, who invented the lyre.

11–13   *Centaur ... Assaracus*: Cheiron the Centaur was the tutor of the young Achilles. Here he prophesies that Achilles will die at Troy, of which Assaracus, great-grandfather of Aeneas, had been king.

XIV

7   *the roller*: the Roman book was a scroll on rollers. 'To reach the roller' therefore means to get to the end of the book.

16   *simmer*: see note on *Odes* I. xiii. 8.

XV

1   *'Twas night*: the lofty tone draws attention to her impiety. Her perjury was committed on a moonlit night when nothing could be hidden.

11–12   *man ... Flaccus ... virtue*: Horace often plays with the etymology of proper names. His own full name is Quintus Horatius Flaccus and *flaccus* is Latin for 'slack'. *Virtus*, Latin 'virtue' is cognate with *vir*, 'man' (see xvi. 39).

21   *Pythagoras*: sixth-century Greek philosopher who believed in reincarnation.

22   *Nireus*: after Achilles, the fairest of the Greeks who came to Troy (*Iliad* ii. 673–4).

XVI

1   *a second generation*: the first would have been those who fought in the war between Pompey and Caesar, which Horace dates as 60–46 BC (see introductory note to *Odes* II. i). Now, sometime in 40–38, their sons seem to be about to begin the civil war fought between Octavian and Sextus Pompeius in 37–36, for which see the note on *Epode* vii.

3–8   The Marsi were defeated in the Social War of 90–89 BC: Capua revolted against Rome after the battle of Cannae in 216 BC in the Second Punic War; Lars Porsena was the Etruscan king who according to one tradition besieged Rome, and according to another captured it, at the end of the seventh century BC; Spartacus was the leader of the slaves in the Servile War of 73–1 BC; the Allobroges were an Alpine people who were in contact with the Catilinarian conspirators in 63 BC and soon afterwards invaded Gaul; the Germans were the Cimbri and Teutones who invaded Italy in 102–101 BC.

14 *the bones of Romulus*: there was a tomb of Romulus in the Roman Forum.

15 *you ask*: here and elsewhere in this poem Horace purports to be addressing an assembly of the Roman people and uses the formal language of the Roman Senate, but there was no Roman assembly which could have been addressed in this way. The pose is that of a political orator, but the scene is not realistic.

18 *Phocaeans*: in 534 BC the people of Phocaea in Asia Minor abandoned their city to escape the Persian yoke (Herodotus i. 165).

28 *The Matine hills*: these, being in the south of Italy, would in normal circumstances have been safe from flooding by the River Po.

41–2 *The Ocean*: Oceanus was believed to be a river encircling the world. Here for the first time in surviving Latin the Isles of the Blest are called the Wealthy Isles.

XVII

Horace is addressing Canidia, the sorceress of *Epodes* iii and v, who is the leader of the Cotytian rites (line 56), which included wholesale sexual indulgence. In these rites Horace (lines 58–9) had been an important figure, but had revealed their secrets (see *Satire* I. iii). He is now at Canidia's mercy, begging for some respite from his punishment. Canidia refuses it, speaking from line 52. His punishment is presumably love. (All the lines in this epode are iambics and it is the only epode of which all the lines are the same metrical length.)

7 *swift wheel*: the magician turned his wheel while uttering prayers and curses (Theocritus ii. 30).

8 *the Nereid's son*: literally grandson of Nereus, god of the sea, that is Achilles, son of the goddess Thetis. Telephus, king of the Mysians, had been wounded by Achilles and was cured by the touch of the spear that had wounded him.

12 *the king*: Priam, king of Troy, who went by night to the camp of the Greeks in the last book of Homer's *Iliad*, and touched the hands which had killed his son. Achilles accepted ransom for Hector's body.

17 *Circe's blessing*: in Homer's *Odyssey* x. 233–43 Circe turns Odysseus' men into pigs. At x. 390–5 she changes them back into men.

20–52 *deceitful lyre*: this part of the poem is heavily ironic. We are to understand from lines 19 and 39 that Canidia is anything but chaste; from line 45 that she is of low birth; from line 46 that at the end of the nine-day mourning period she collects pauper's bones for her magic spells and potions; from line 48 that she does not respect the laws of hospitality (we think of the fifth *Epode*), and that she is sterile and pretends to have babies, in order to stand well with her lovers.

27–8 *Sabellan . . . Marsian*: peoples of central Italy famous for expertise in magic.

30 *Hercules*: see note on iii. 17.

41 *Castor*: Castor and Pollux blinded Stesichorus when he wrote a poem attacking their sister Helen. His sight was restored when he wrote a palinode.

55 *Cotytian rites*: Cotys was a Thracian goddess.

59 *Paelignian*: the Paelignians were another people of central Italy famous for their skill in magic.

71 *Noric*: from Noricum in the Alps, famous for the excellence of its steel.

ODES, BOOK I

I

Horace's ambition is that his patron Maecenas will think his name worthy to be added to the canon of the nine great lyric poets of Greece. Lines 3–6 allude to Pindar's epinician Odes in praise of the victors in the Greek games. Line 34 refers to his other vital inspiration, the poetry of Sappho and Alcaeus of Lesbos.

This poem consists of a cheerful sketch of nine different ways of life, of which the last is his own. His suggestion is that his own passion is just like the others, with ivy instead of the palm and with the grove instead of the arbutus, the strawberry tree of line 21. He is not raised by the whim of the Roman people, but rather set apart from the people by Nymphs and Satyrs, and hoping to be raised to the stars by the judgement of Maecenas. He is not involved in the stormy seas of the Greek world, the Myrtoan and the Icarian, but with the poets of Lesbos and Olympian odes of Pindar. Horace is smiling at himself, but is serious.

8 *triple honours*: quaestorship, praetorship, consulship.

13 *Attalus*: bequeathed his kingdom of Pergamum to the Roman people in 133 BC.

14–16 *Myrtoan . . . Icarian*: Roman poets like to particularize. The Myrtoan sea, notorious for its storms, lies to the east of the Peloponnese. The Icarian is more remote, in the eastern Aegean round the island of Icaria.

33–4 *Euterpe . . . Polyhymnia*: two of the nine Muses. Later, when the Muses were allocated to separate arts, these two became responsible for pipe-playing and sacred song respectively. Pipes would be thought of as accompanying choral music like the odes of Pindar; stringed instruments could be played by the poet accompanying his own song.

II

The dramatic date of this poem is some time after the battle of Actium in 31 BC, after which Octavian took over from Antony the control of the East (lines 51–2). To narrow it down, the only recorded flood of the Tiber in that period (lines 13–20) was on 16–17 January 27 BC (Dio Cassius liii. 4–8). This was three days after Augustus had given up his extraordinary constitutional powers and caused consternation by proposing to retire into private life. At this same time he received the title of Leader of the Senate, *Princeps Senatus* (line 50).

5 *Pyrrha*: Pyrrha and her husband Deucalion were the two mortals who survived the Flood (Ovid, *Metamorphoses* i. 348–415).

15–18 *Numa . . . Vesta . . . Ilia*: Numa was the second king of Rome, said to have built the Regia, the residence the Chief Priest, *Pontifex Maximus*, and the round temple of Vesta (lines 15–16). Julius Caesar was *Pontifex Maximus* at the time of his assassination in 44 BC. Ilia (18), raped by Mars, and mother of Romulus and Remus, now wife of the River Tiber, was a member of the Julian family descended from Iulus, son of Aeneas, and an ancestor of Julius Caesar. Hence in line 17 her grievances and her husband's indignation. This passage therefore alludes to the portents observed before the assassination, which led to the civil wars which ended at Philippi and Actium. Now in 27 BC Horace is praying that similar portents will not lead to similar results and that Augustus, the contemporary Julian, the first *Princeps*, will be spared to govern Rome for many long triumphant years.

22 *Persian enemies*: the Parthians.

26–52 *What prayer . . . leader*: this passage contains many of the features of the standard hymn form—the address to a god, sometimes without using the god's name, the repetition of the second person pronoun, the functions and attributes of the god, the shrine (33), the retinue (34), names and parentage (41), before the actual prayer (see 45–52).

33   *Eryx*: at the north-west tip of Sicily is one of many shrines of Venus, mother of Aeneas, mentioned here because it is the site of the tomb of Anchises, father of Aeneas, whose contemporary descendants, Julius Caesar and Augustus, are the subjects of this ode.

37   *the god of war*: Mars, also attached to the Julian family tree (see note on 15–18).

44   *Caesar' avenger*: Octavian, grand-nephew and heir of Julius Caesar, started his climb to power by promising Caesar's soldiers that he would avenge his death. In due course he kept his promise and saw to the death of all the conspirators.

47   *no breeze*: Horace prays that Augustus will not be like Romulus. Livy I. xvi. 2 tells how he was snatched up by the wind and never seen on earth again.

III

Horace's friend Virgil is sailing to Greece and Horace calls upon his ship to carry him safely. This leads to a condemnation of the first sailor, and thence to the impious daring of men, and Jupiter's punishment of it.

1–4   Cyprus is the home of Venus. The brothers of Helen are Castor and Pollux, who calm the seas when they appear at the mastheads of ships in the form of a blue incandescence now known as St Elmo's Fire. The father of the winds is Aeolus, who rules them in a cave in the Aeolian islands.

14   *Hyades*: a constellation which brings rain at its rising and its setting.

20   *Acroceraunian rocks*: a promontory on the north-west coast of Greece opposite the heel of Italy, where Octavian's ship lost its rigging and broke its rudder in a storm after Actium.

27   *Iapetus*: father of Prometheus, who brought down fire to mortals in a fennel stick.

34   *Daedalus*: escaped from the Labyrinth he had built for Minos, king of Crete, by making wings of feathers attached with wax (Ovid, *Metamorphoses* viii. 183–235). When his son Icarus flew too close to the sun, the wax melted and he fell into the sea which took his name.

40   *thunderbolts*: the thunderbolts of Jupiter are associated with the Civil Wars at I. ii. 2–3, I. xii. 59–60, and III. iv. 44.

IV

14 *Sestius*: Lucius Sestius fought for Brutus against Octavian at Philippi in 42 BC, was amnestied, and became part of the Augustan establishment, taking over the consulship from Augustus in 23 BC. The fourth poem in this collection published in that year is thus the fourth to honour prominent figures in the Augustan regime. The Sestii were rich (in line 14 the word *beate* means fortunate, blessed, wealthy). They owned potteries near Cosa on the Etruscan coast 140 km. north-west of Rome. From its port their ships would start sailing every spring with cargoes of amphorae filled with wine, oil and fish products. These potteries were known as *officinae* and *officinae* is the word used for foundries in line 8 of the ode. The name of this Sestius and the letters OF for *officina* appear on bricks made in these potteries. The Sestii had connections with the turreted villa of *Sette Finestre* at Cosa (14), no doubt more spacious than Pluto's meagre house in the Underworld in line 17.

V

This is the most famous of Horace's odes. Sir Ronald Storrs collected 451 version of it in 21 languages, of which 144 were published under the title of *Ad Pyrrham* in 1959. The tally keeps rising. The poem plays upon the ancient practice whereby on retirement the huntsman would dedicate his nets to Diana and the prostitute her mirror to Venus. The miracles of the poem include its music, the many details of interplay between storms at sea and the storms of love, and the typical Horatian twist that Horace's first love poem in this collection is a farewell to one type of love.

VI

The *recusatio* is an established form in Latin poetry. It enables the poet to compliment two people in one poem, by declining to praise a patron on the grounds of incapacity, and suggesting someone who could do it better (see Lyne, 31–9). So here Horace declines to write in praise of Augustus and Marcus Agrippa, his great admiral, general, and engineer, on the grounds that he is only a love poet. He puts forward instead the name of his friend Varius, epic poet and tragedian, who wrote a *Thyestes* about the house of Pelops (line 8), and was richly rewarded for it by Augustus.

6–7 *bad temper . . . double-dealer*: Horace flaunts his incompetence by trivializing his allusions to the anger of Achilles and the wanderings of Odysseus, the themes of Homer's *Iliad* and *Odyssey*.

13–16 Horace now shows that he can do the Big Bow-Wow strain as well as the next man.

VII

6–7 *Pallas . . . olive*: Pallas Athena was the virgin goddess of Athens and the olive tree was her gift to the city.

9–12 This stanza alludes to the Greek heroes in the *Iliad*, Mycenae being the home of Agamemnon, Argos of Diomede, Lacedaemon (Sparta) of Menelaus, and, according to Virgil *Aeneid* ii. 197, Larisa of Achilles.

12–13 *Albunea . . . Tiburnus*: Albunea was the Sibyl of Tibur, and Tiburnus its founder hero. Tibur (modern Tivoli) was a town in the hills 40 km. east of Rome, by falls of the River Anio, where wealthy Romans, perhaps including Plancus (see line 21, and notes on 17 and 23) had their villas.

17 *Plancus*: Titus Munatius Plancus had been governor of Asia Minor under Antony in the early thirties BC, but had gone over to Octavian when Antony allowed Cleopatra to be present in the campaign which led to the battle of Actium. If the dramatic date of this poem is set in that period, the situation of Plancus corresponds in several ways to that of Teucer, whose father, Telamon of Salamis, drove him into exile on his return from the Trojan War.

23 *poplar*: emblem of Hercules, god of Tibur, who appears on a coin of the city minted by Plancus.

29 *a second Salamis*: Teucer founded a new Salamis in Cyprus.

VIII

2 *Sybaris*: male lovers in the odes are often given Greek names when the context makes it clear that they are thought of as Romans. So here, although his name suggests that Sybaris is a citizen of the notoriously luxurious and licentious Greek city of Sybaris in the south of Italy, he is, or should be, training for military service on the Campus Martius. He is therefore thought of as a young Roman.

13 *Thetis*: in a vain attempt to keep her son Achilles from the Trojan War, Thetis hid him on the island of Scyros dressed as a girl.

IX

1 *Soracte*: a mountain 32 km. north of Rome on the borders of the Sabine country (7).

6 *Thaliarchus*: in Greek 'Banquet-master', presumably Horace's
   slave, cupbearer and boy lover. Ganymede, the cupbearer of
   Jupiter, has given us the word 'catamite'. The end of the poem
   suggests that, like Lycidas at the end of I. iv, Thaliarchus is about
   to move on to fresh fields.

X

A hymn to Mercury, messenger of the gods, brother of Apollo, with
some of the hymn features observed on I. ii. 26–52. Another common
hymn feature is the adjective clause attached to the address, as in line 2.

6 *lyre*: Mercury's first act was to invent the lyre by killing a tortoise
   and stringing its shell with sheep-gut (Homeric *Hymn to Hermes*
   24–55).

13 *Priam*: Mercury (in Greek Hermes) escorted the aged king Priam
   through the army of the Greeks, laden with ransom to offer
   Achilles in exchange for the body of his son Hector (*Iliad* xxiv.
   332–469, see note on *Epode* xvii. 12).

XI

A dramatic monologue. The hint is that Leuconoe has told Horace that
she has consulted an astrologer because she has a premonition that he,
or she, is about to die.

5 *the Tyrrhenian sea*: to the west of Italy. Pumice is congealed lava
   and is found on the Italian seashore only in the volcanic regions of
   the south round the bay of Naples.

8 *Harvest the day*: the Latin is *Carpe diem*. With the talk of wine and
   of pruning (surely of the vine), the final metaphor recommends
   regular daily picking of the grapes, wine-drinking, and love-
   making.

XII

1 *Clio*: one of the Muses, later associated with history. According to
   Eustathius on *Iliad* x. 442 she was mother of Orpheus (see line 9).
   The opening of this poem announces Horace's devotion to Pindar,
   who begins his second Olympian 'Hymns that rule the lyre, what
   god, what hero, what man shall we proclaim? Zeus is lord of
   Pisa . . .'

5–6 *Helicon . . . Pindus . . . Haemus*: famous Greek mountains, Heli-
   con being the mountain of the Muses, Haemus in Thrace being
   associated with Orpheus.

13 *custom*: as, for example, 'Let us begin with Zeus, Muses, and let us end with Zeus' (Theocritus xvii. 1), a precept followed in this poem.

22 *bold in battle*: for the prowess in war of the god of wine see II. xix. 21–4.

    virgin goddess: a common feature of the hymn form is the reference to Diana without mention of her name (cf. note on I. ii. 26–42).

25–6 *the sons of Leda*: as the ode moves from Greek gods to Greek heroes, it also moves towards Rome. There was a tradition (Dionysius of Halicarnassus VI. xiii. 1–2) that Castor and Pollux, sons of Leda and Tyndareus, were present at the battle of Lake Regillus in 496 BC and brought the news of the victory to Rome. For their function as gods of sailors see note on I. iii. 1–4.

33–6 *Romulus . . . Pompilius . . . Tarquin . . . Cato*: just as the first stanza surveys Greek topics, so this pivotal ninth stanza takes in a sweep of Roman history from the first two kings, Romulus and Pompilius Numa, through the last, Tarquinius Superbus, who usurped the *fasces*, the rods of office, and was expelled in 510 BC, to the last of the republican heroes Cato the Younger (95–46 BC), who committed suicide after his defeat at Thapsus.

37–52 In answer to his own question in line 33, Horace in line 37 begins a litany of heroes of the Roman Republic, culminating in C. Claudius Marcellus, consul five times at the end of the third century BC. This leads smoothly to the contemporary Marcellus of the same name, who married Augustus' daughter Julia in 25 BC. Lines 46–8 acclaim his joining the Julian family by the reference to the comet which appeared at the games held by Octavian/Augustus after the assassination of Julius Caesar.

XIII

8 *macerating*: 'cooking on a slow heat'. By the extended cooking metaphor (from lines 4 to 8 or 9), Horace mocks his own jealousy and the excesses of love poets, including the famous list of the detailed symptoms of love in Sappho fragment 31 and Catullus 51. The same word, *macerare*, occurs to similar effect in *Epode* xiv. 16. See note on III. xix. 28 and IV. i. 9–10.

XIV

1 *O ship*: Horace is inspired by poems in which Alcaeus appears to address the Ship of State (fragments 6 and 28). The dramatic date of the ode is some time when the Civil Wars were breaking out

again (lines 1 and 10) after they had seemed to be over, perhaps at a time when Augustus' life was in danger.

18 *longing*: the Latin is *desiderium*, used of Romulus in Ennius *Annales* 105 (see note on IV. v. 1–8) and of Augustus at *Odes* IV. v. 15.

XV

1–2 *the shepherd . . . Idaean*: Paris, son of Priam, had been a shepherd on Mount Ida, near Troy. On a visit to Sparta he fell in love with Helen, wife of Menelaus. Here the sea god Nereus prophesies the Trojan War. Ambiguity and obscurity are of great assistance to prophets, and here Horace suggests the oracular style with 'the shepherd', the 'dragging across the sea', and the withholding of the words 'Paris' and 'Troy'.

19–27 *Ajax's . . . Tydeus*: all the names in this passage are of Greek heroes at the siege of Troy. The son of Laertes is Odysseus, whose device, the Wooden Horse, led to the taking of the city. The son of Tydeus is Diomede, the greatest warrior of the Greeks, who rages at Paris after Paris' arrow has struck his foot at *Iliad* xi. 368–95.

33 *the anger of Achilles' fleet*: more oracular obscurity. It was not the fleet that postponed the fall of Troy, but the anger of Achilles.

XVI

2 *iambics*: in his youth Horace had written scurrilous poems about his mistress in the iambic metre (compare some of his *Epodes*) and now he apologizes, recants, and asks her to love him again.

5–10 Dindymus is a mountain in Phrygia, sacred to the goddess Cybele; Delphi is the shrine of Apollo; Liber the god of wine, Bacchus; the Corybantes are the priests of Cybele, here identified with the Curetes of Crete who clashed cymbals to drown the cries of the baby Zeus while they hid him from the murderous intentions of his father Cronos. For Noricum see note on *Epode* xvii. 71. The overblown language hints that Horace is not speaking in total seriousness.

17 *Thyestes*: see note on *Epode* v. 86.

XVII

1 *Faunus*: the Latin Faunus, god of the countryside, corresponds to the Greek Pan, the wolf god, in Greek *Lyceios* (see line 9). It is an easy journey from Mount Lycaeus in Arcadia to Mount Lucretilis (note typical Horatian word-play) near the Sabine estate which

Horace had received from his patron Maecenas some time about 33 BC.

13–16 *my Muse . . . plenty*: the centre of the Horatian ode is often load-bearing. This stanza is Horace's way of thanking Maecenas for the Sabine estate.

17–28 The ode ends with a specimen of the love poetry Horace is writing in the Sabine country. Part of the fun is the host of correspondences between the pleasures of Horace's goats and the joys promised to Tyndaris.

18–20 *Teian*: Anacreon of Teos wrote poems of love and wine. Here Horace thinks of such a poem about the love affairs of Odysseus.

22 *Thyonian*: according to the usual myth the mother of Bacchus was Semele, but one version holds that it was Thyone, a daughter of the Hyades. Horace may be tempted by this version here because the Greek word *thuo* means 'I rage'.

XVIII

Dionysus, the Greek god of wine, is praised under his Latin names, Bacchus and Liber, and under his orgiastic Greek titles, Euhius and Bassareus.

2 *Catilus*: one of the co-founders of Tibur with Tiburnus (see note on I. vii. 13).

7 *Lapiths*: fought with Centaurs at the wedding of Pirithous and Laodamia in Thessaly in north Greece, depicted on the Parthenon frieze in the British Museum, which Horace could have seen as a student in Athens (see note on I. xxvii. 6).

9 *Thracians*: also from north Greece. Northerners were notorious for their drunkenness.

11 *shake*: perhaps a reference to rituals in which a god is taken from his shrine in a sacred basket to be carried in procession.

14 *Berecyntian horn*: a Phrygian double pipe, used in orgiastic rites. One of the two pipes was a bass with a curved end.

16 *Trust*: the Romans valued confidentiality in their drinking companions (see Ennius, *Annales* 268–85).

XIX

11 *Scythians . . . Parthian horsemen*: famous for their Parthian shots, arrows delivered in retreat.

XX

1   *plain . . . ordinary*: the simplicity of what Horace offers Maecenas is a coded statement of his confidence in Maecenas' friendship, of his gratitude for the Sabine estate, and of his contentment. He will not be asking for more. See I. xvii. 14–16.

2   *Greek jar*: the jar which had held the superior wine will raise the quality of the modest Sabine.

3   *the day*: when Maecenas made his first public appearance in the theatre after an illness the audience rose to acclaim him.

6   *the river*: the Tiber was known as the Tuscan river because Etruria lay on its right bank. Maecenas was thought to be descended from Etruscan kings (I. i. 1 and III. xxix. 1).

9–12   These four wines were produced near the mouth of the River Liris. The first two wines came from its north side in Latium; the others from the south in Campania. The Sabine hills produced a much rougher drink. This is a coded statement of Horace's sturdy independence.

XXI

2–3   *Cynthius . . . Latona*: Latona gave birth to Apollo and Diana on Mount Cynthus in Delos. For Apollo see note on I. xxxi. 1.

7–10   Erymanthus is a mountain in Arcadia, Gragos in Lycia, and Tempe is a beautiful valley in Thessaly. Mount Algidus, some 30 km. south-east of Rome, near Velitrae, the birthplace of Augustus, establishes the interest of Diana in things Italian.

14–15   *Caesar the Princeps*: the Italian connection having just been established, Horace now prays for Augustus. For the title *Princeps* see I. ii. 50.

15   *to the Persians*: it strengthened a prayer to be rid of something, if the supplicant suggested where the god should send it, for example 'Raine, raine, goe to Spain'.

XXII

2   *Fuscus*: the teasing of Horace by Aristius Fuscus at *Satires* I. ix. 60–74 alerts us to the possibility that this ode may not be entirely serious.

6   *Syrtes*: the lofty Stoic tone of the opening points to Cato's famous march of 47 BC across the desert Syrtes in north Africa, over a thousand km. in thirty days.

8   *Hydaspes*: the River Hydaspes in the Punjab was the scene of a
    famous victory of Alexander the Great in 326 BC.

13 *Daunia*: the kingdom founded by the legendary king Daunus, a
    district in the northern part of Apulia in south-west Italy. It in-
    cluded Venusia, Horace's birthplace.

15 *Juba*: king of Mauretania. We are not expected to believe that a
    wolf larger than any Moroccan lion turned and ran when it heard
    Horace singing of his Lalage, certainly not when the desert is called
    a dry nurse.

XXIII

9   *Gaetulian lion*: the Gaetulians lived just south of Mauretania.

XXIV

3   *Melpomene*: a Muse, later associated with tragedy. The Muses were
    daughters of Zeus.

6   *Quintilius*: a friend of Horace and trusted critic of his work (See *Ars
    Poetica* 438–44).

13 *Thracian Orpheus*: In *Georgics* iv. 467–503 Virgil had tuned his lyre
    to sing of Orpheus' descent into the Underworld in a vain attempt
    to rescue his wife Eurydice from death.

XXV

14 *the mothers of horses*: mares were notoriously lustful, and the lofty
    tone of the passage may be a glance at Virgil *Georgics* iii. 266–79,
    where their behaviour is vividly described.

XXVI

3   *what king*: a possible answer would be the Dacian Cotiso, who was
    causing trouble on the Danube in 30 BC (III. viii. 18, *Satires* II. vi.
    53).

5   *Tiridates*: must often have known fear between 31 and 26 BC when
    he twice rebelled and twice took the throne of Parthia. He was
    eventually expelled and fled to the Romans.

6   *Pimpleis*: the Muse, from Pimpla, a town near the Pierian fountain
    of the Muses on Mount Olympus.

8   *Lamia*: perhaps Lucius Aelius Lamia, legate in Spain in 26–25 BC.

XXVII

6 *Persian dagger*: this is a dramatic monologue. The dashes indicate where we are to imagine words spoken by the young men drinking with Horace. For example, before the poem begins a row has developed and someone is waving a Persian dagger. One such dagger, an *acinaces*, was kept in the Parthenon as a relic of the Persian Wars. Horace must have seen it there in his student days in Athens, and so would the young men he pretends to be addressing. We are perhaps to imagine that one of them had bought one as a souvenir, and taken it along to the symposium. The poem opens with an appeal by Horace to the standards of behaviour of the civilized west as opposed to the barbarous practices of the north and east (see notes on I. xviii. 7 and 9).

10 *Opys*: there were two places of this name in Greece, but this symposium seems to be a meeting of young Romans, and Horace does on occasion, as with Sybaris in I. viii, give young Romans Greek names and connections.

19 *Charybdis*: a whirlpool in Homer's *Odyssey* xii, and hence a name for a prostitute.

21–2 *witch . . . magician . . . god*: another play upon the opening of Pindar's second Olympian. See note on I. xii. 1.

24 *Chimaera*: a monster of rapacity with a lion's head, a snake's tail, and its own body, and hence a name for a prostitute.

XXVIII

This is a dramatic monologue, more complex than I. xxvii. At the tomb of Archytas the speaker is brooding on the inevitability of death. It is not till line 21 that we learn that he is already dead. The rest of the poem is his appeal, to a passing sailor, to throw a little sand over his body. Its tone is first ingratiating, then threatening, then pleading.

2 *Archytas*: fourth-century BC mathematician and Pythagorean philosopher. There is no evidence that he counted the number of grains of sand in the world (that achievement belonged to Archimedes), but poignant although it is in this context, it need not be false. Horace knew more about Archytas than we do.

7–15 Four Greeks who died although they had some claim to immortality: Tantalus, father of Pelops, dined with the gods and tasted ambrosia; Tithonus was loved by Eos, the goddess of the dawn, and her chariot carried him off into the winds (Statius, *Silvae* I. ii.

44-5); Minos, king of Crete, held conversations with Zeus every nine years (Homer, *Odyssey* xix. 178-9); Pythagoras believed he was a reincarnation of the Greek hero Euphorbus, son of Panthoos, and proved it by recognizing his shield dedicated on a temple wall in Argos. When it was taken down the name of Euphorbus was found inscribed inside it.

21-9 In a dramatic monologue one has to reconstruct the setting from details planted by the poet. Here the speaker is a corpse washed up on the shore presumably at or near Tarentum in south Italy, where Archytas had been seven times elected ruler, *strategos*. The Matine shore (3) may also be on the bay of Tarentum (*Epode* xvi. 28). The passing sailor seems also to be a Tarentine (29), on a trip to Greece, about to turn north into the Adriatic, the Illyrian sea (21), and meet the headwinds from the east (25), which will impede his crossing to Greece. These same winds will continue westwards and toss the trees in the woods of Horace's homeland at Venusia (27).

XXIX

1 *Iccius*: a young friend of Horace in whose mind there seems from *Epistles* I. xii to have been a conflict between a love of philosophy and a love of money.

2-3 *Arabia . . . Sheba*: in 26-25 BC an expedition was mounted against Arabia to attempt to take over the revenues exacted by the Shebans from the spice trade.

5 *Mede*: the theatre of war has moved unexpectedly to the Parthians, the Medes as they were called in poetry. Perhaps in this context Horace is evoking the Persian Wars, as in I. ii. 22, as the archetypal conflict between civilization and barbarism.

9 *by your cup*: the cupbearer is often the boy lover, as in I. ix, and his long, unshorn hair a treasured mark of his youth.

14 *Panaetius*: Stoic philosopher influential in Rome in the second half of the second century BC. He held Socrates in high regard.

XXX

A hymn with many of the features noted on I. ii. 26-42.

8 *Mercury*: as ever in Horace, the names of the gods have to be read with a feeling of what they stand for. Mercury is the god of eloquence, fun, civilization, inventor of the lyre (I. x), companion of Venus (*Epistles* I. vi. 38), and protector of Horace (II. vii. 13, and xvii. 29).

XXXI

1 *Apollo*: on 9 October 28 BC Augustus dedicated the glorious new temple of Apollo adjoining his own house on the Palatine. Apollo, son of Jupiter and Latona, was the god of music, medicine, prophecy, and archery, and the giver of the victory at Actium. This ode celebrates this climax of the Augustan regime by immediately making it clear that the beginning of the Augustan Age was a time when the poet was given space to praise as he wished (see next note).

3 *new wine*: on 11 October, two days after the dedication of the temple of Apollo, came the festival of the new wine, the Meditrinalia, on which was chanted the ancient formula, 'I drink wine new and old. I heal disease new and old.' Horace has glided from the god of the state to the personal god who gives him his health and his poetry (see lines 18–20).

16 *olives*: the simple diet is no doubt literal, but it is also a code for Horace's simple life and non-bombastic poetry.

XXXII

3 *Greek . . . Latin*: his proudest boast is that he has brought Greek lyric poetry to Rome (see I. i. 33–6 and III. xxx. 13–14).

5 *citizen of Lesbos*: Alcaeus wrote of war, of the ship of state in storm (see note on I. xiv. 1), of wine, and of love.

XXXIII

1 *Albius*: Albius Tibullus, elegiac poet, teased affectionately for his melancholy in *Epistles* I. iv, author of two elegies lamenting the faithlessness of his mistress Delia.

XXXIV

3 *wisdom*: followers of Epicurus called his philosophy Wisdom, *Sapientia*. Basic tenets were that the gods did not interfere in human affairs, that everything in the world was caused by physical events at atomic level. Lightning, for example, is the expulsion of concentrated atoms of heat from clouds. This is argued with characteristic detail, passion, and sublimity by Lucretius in *De Rerum Natura* vi. 160–218, and theological explanations are derided in lines 379–422.

8 *cloudless sky*: Horace's Epicurean beliefs are shattered by the sound of lightning from a clear sky—or so he claims. He therefore reverts

to the theological explanation in terms which repeatedly expropriate the language of Lucretius.

10 *Taenarus*: on Cape Taenarus (now Matapan) there was a cave which was supposed to give entry to the Underworld.

12 *God*: once again is seen as the ruler of human life, and here is equated with Fortune, unpredictable, unpitying, and malicious.

XXXV

1 *Goddess*: as so often in this book one ode refers back to the one before. This is a hymn to the goddess Fortuna of Antium on the coast south of Rome, 29 km. from Augustus' birthplace, Velitrae (see note on I. xxi. 7-10). This temple benefited from the generosity of Octavian after it supported him in the Perusine War of 41-40 BC (Appian v. xxiv. 97), and perhaps in the early twenties, when he was refurbishing the temples of Rome.

6-7 *Carpathian . . . Bithynian*: Carpathos was an island in the eastern Mediterranean south-west of Rhodes. Bithynia was on the south coast of the Black Sea. The adjectives are typical of Horace in that they particularize, and also are relevant, because of their remoteness, to the argument of the poem (cf. I. i. 14).

17-22 The vivid imagery of the iconography of the goddess suggests that such figures could be seen in the decoration of the temple at Antium as refurbished with the help of Octavian/Augustus. Priests in the Roman temple of *Fides*, here translated as Loyalty, had their hands swathed in white cloth according to Livy I. xxi. 4.

21-8 This passage is difficult to understand. When Fortune abandons a man, Loyalty goes with her, and hangers-on (25-8) also leave the house.

30-2 *Britain . . . East and the Red Sea*: in 27-26 BC Augustus planned expeditions to Britain. These are also the years of the Arabian expedition of I. xxix. 2-3.

40 *Massagetae*: the diatribe against the Civil Wars ends with the 'Rain to Spain' motif (see note on I. xxi. 15), but this time the prayer is that the evil may smite Arabia and this Scythian tribe far away beyond the Caspian Sea.

XXXVI

4 *Numida*: unknown and unimportant. The poem is a tribute to the Lamia of I. xxvi.

9 *the toga*: when a Roman boy reached the age of 15, he shaved his beard, cut his hair, and donned the toga of manhood, *toga virilis*.

10   *chalk*: see note on IV. iv. 39.

12   *Salii*: priests of Mars famous for their dancing in triple time and their lavish feasts.

13–14 *Damalis . . . Bassus*: presumably Damalis is Numida's lover, and Bassus is a friend of Numida's, but no friend of wine. For Thracians see note on I. xviii. 9.

XXXVII

3   *couches*: at *lectisternia*, effigies of the gods were set on couches outside their temples and laden tables were set before them while their worshippers feasted with them *al fresco*.

4   *Salian*: see note on I. xxxvi. 12.

7   *contaminated flock*: an allusion to the eunuchs at the court of the Ptolemies.

9   *ruin of the Capitol*: Cleopatra's oath (Dio Cassius l. 5) was 'as surely as I shall sit on the Capitol in judgement'.

14   *Mareotic wine*: a sweet Egyptian wine. This touches on the entertainments Cleopatra provided for Antony in the years before Actium, a familiar theme of Octavian's propaganda.

15   *real fears*: the stock account of the battle holds that the crucial moment came when Cleopatra panicked needlessly and took to flight, to be followed by her lover.

18   *swift*: history is telescoped. The battle was fought on 2 September 31 BC. Cleopatra died on 10 August 30 BC, a few days after Antony.

31   *Liburnians*: see note on *Epode* i. 1.

XXXVIII

After the Augustan panegyric of I. xxxvii, Horace pointedly ends with a little poem of wine and love.

6   *myrtle*: associated with Venus at I. xxv. 18 and II. vii. 25.

7   *cupbearer*: for cupbearers see notes on I. ix. 6 and xxix. 9.

ODES, BOOK II

I

The first 32 lines of this poem seem to allude to details of the lost history of the Civil Wars by Gaius Asinius Pollio (76 BC–AD 4). This probably accounts for the prosaic beginning which dates the unrest from the

consulship of Quintus Metellus Celer in 60 BC, when Caesar and
Pompey formed an alliance, the year before they were joined by Crassus
in the First Triumvirate. These were all to die violent deaths, thus
illustrating the danger of the friendships of the great, grievous to them-
selves and to Rome (see lines 3-4). Pollio was on Caesar's staff in 49 BC
and crossed the Rubicon with him. He may even have heard him
quoting Menander 'The die is cast' (line 6). He fought at Caesar's side
at Pharsalus in 48 BC when Caesar ordered his hardened cavalrymen to
aim at the faces of the young gentlemen opposing them (line 20), and no
doubt was present when Caesar and his staff officers, caked with the
dust and sweat of battle, met after Pharsalus believing that their victory
had ended the Civil War (lines 21-3). But the Pompeians continued
their fight in Africa, inspired by Cato the Younger, the archetypal
republican, until the defeat at Thapsus in 46 BC, after which Cato
committed suicide rather than live under Caesar (lines 23-8). Pollio was
a lover of peace (lines 29-36), and even in these turbulent years he was
writing tragedy (line 12), as we learn from three surviving letters he
wrote to Cicero in 43 BC (*Ad. Fam.* x. 31-3). After the assassination of
Caesar he served under Antony and won a triumph against the Parthini
in 39 or 38 BC (lines 15-16). This was the end of his military career.
From this date onwards he devoted himself largely to literature, acting
as a patron of poets, creating a library in Rome, and establishing the
practice of public readings (lines 17 and 21).

2   *its evils and the ways of it*: this list of contents, and some of the terms
    in it, resemble the opening chapters of other Roman historians and
    may carry allusions to the proem of Pollio's *Historiae*.

12   *the buskin of Cecrops*: Cecrops was the legendary founder king of
    Athens, and the buskin was the high boot worn by tragic actors.

14   *consulting you*: as consul in 40 BC Pollio would have consulted the
    Senate. This paradox is a flattering allusion to his role as senior
    statesman.

27   *descendants of the victors*: members of the Scipio family led Roman
    armies which captured Carthage after the battle of Zama in 202 BC
    and destroyed it in 146 BC. In 109 BC Quintus Caecilius Metellus
    took a prominent part in the defeat of Jugurtha, king of Numidia,
    a kingdom lying to the west of Carthage. Now at the battle of
    Thapsus in 46 BC all this was avenged when Quintus Metellus Pius
    Scipio, grandson by adoption of that same Metellus, led Romans to
    defeat by Romans.

31   *Hesperia*: the land of the west. By referring to Italy by this poetic
    term and to the Parthians as the Medes, Horace implies that Rome

has inherited from Greece the role of champion of Western civilization against Oriental barbarism (see note on I. xxvii. 6 and xxix. 5).

35 *Daunians*: Horace thinks of his own compatriots from the south of Italy who died in the Civil Wars. See note on I. xxii. 13.

38 *Cean dirges*: Ceos was the home of Simonides.

39 *Dione*: mother of Venus.

II

3 *Crispus Sallustius*: inherited from his great-uncle the historian Sallust great wealth, a splendid house, and famous gardens in Rome. He also owned copper mines in the Alps. He was a generous patron of literature and succeeded Maecenas as Augustus' most trusted minister.

5 *Proculeius*: another member of Augustus' entourage.

11 *both Carthages*: Horace satirizes the desire of landowners to join up their properties by this absurd notion of linking Libya to Gades (Cadiz, just west of the Strait of Gibraltar), and Carthage in Libya to New Carthage on the south-east tip of Spain.

17 *Phraates . . . Cyrus*: Phraates, king of Parthia, was twice deposed (in 31 and 26 BC) by the Roman puppet Tiridates (see note on I. xxvi. 5), and twice regained his throne. Cyrus was the legendary 'good' king of Persia, here, as in the previous poem, equated with Parthia.

III

3 *Dellius*: Quintus Dellius was famous for his full participation in the delights of Cleopatra's court while serving under Antony and for his readiness to change sides in the Civil Wars, but is now, like Pollio, Sallustius, and Proculeius, a member of the Augustan circle. The choice of addressees in several of the odes in this book advertises the Augustan policy of reconciliation after Actium.

8 *Falernian*: while in Alexandria with Antony Dellius teased Cleopatra by telling her that Egyptian wine was no match for Falernian. In this poem it looks as though Horace is 'recommending hedonism to a hedonist' (Nisbet and Hubbard, 52).

16 *three sisters*: the Fates, who spin threads for the lives of men; when they cut the thread, the man dies.

22 *Inachus*: first king of Argos, whose descendants colonized Italy.

IV

1 *Phocian Xanthus*: although Phocis is in Greece and the boy has a
Greek name, he may still be thought of as a Roman (see note on I.
viii. 2).

2–12 Achilles, Ajax, son of Telamon, and Agamemnon, son of Atreus,
were all Greek heroes at the siege of Troy. The anger of Achilles,
the Thessalian of line 10, arose when Agamemnon deprived him of
his captive Briseis. After the sack of the city Agamemnon carried
off the Trojan princess Cassandra, who had been raped by Ajax,
son of Oileus.

VI

1 *Septimius*: mentioned in *Epistles* I. ix, otherwise unknown.

2 *Cantabrian*: a ferocious people on the north coast of Spain, who
repeatedly rose against Rome in the twenties.

5 *Tibur*: see note on I. vii. 13 and I. xviii. 2.

12 *Phalanthus*: the founder of Tarentum, from Sparta in Laconia.

15 *Hymettus*: the hill near Athens famous for its honey.

16 *Venafrum*: in Samnium in central Italy on the River Volturnus.

22 *citadels*: the towers of the citadel of Tarentum are mentioned by
Virgil at *Georgics* iv. 125.

VII

1 *Pompeius*: unknown, but from the poem we can deduce that he
fought alongside Horace in Brutus' army at the battle of Philippi in
42 BC, and may guess that thereafter he continued to campaign
against Octavian until the amnesty after Actium (see lines 3–4 and
21). Being a Pompeius, he may well have fought in sea battles for
Sextus Pompeius until his defeat in 36 BC (see lines 15–16).

10 *my little shield*: Archilochus, Alcaeus, and Anacreon all claim to
have thrown away their shields in battle.

11 *virtue . . . chins*: a calculated ambiguity. Horace seems to be admit-
ting that he had been guilty of over-confidence and had been forced
to capitulate, but he is also suggesting criticism of Brutus, who was
notorious for his stoic Virtue and his immodesty in proclaiming it.
Roman aristocrats did submit to Octavian after Philippi (Appian
iv. 135).

13 *swift Mercury*: Mercury is not one of the great Olympians who
rescued their favourites from the battlefield in the *Iliad*. He is more

lightweight, a proper patron for someone as unimportant as Horace (II. xvii. 29).

21 *Egyptian cups*: *ciboria*, perhaps mementoes, if Pompeius had been with Antony in Egypt after Actium.

25 *myrtle . . . Venus*: myrtle is the plant of Venus and a Venus is the highest throw on the dice.

26 *Edonian*: a Thracian tribe in whose territory was fought the battle of Philippi. The Edonians are Maenads taking part in the orgiastic rites of Bacchus in Propertius I. iii. 5 and Ovid *Metamorphoses* xi. 69.

VIII

3–4 *white on a fingernail*: the sign of a liar.
22 *bullocks*: see II. v. 1–9 and 15–16.

IX

5 *Valgius*: a friend of Horace's. Horace is advising him that he has written too many poems about his dead slave boy Mystes, and urges him instead to write in praise of Augustus.

13 *the old man*: Nestor, father of Antilochus.

X

1 *Licinius*: perhaps Licinius Murena, brother-in-law of Maecenas, accused of conspiracy against Augustus in 23 or 22 BC.

5 *the Golden Mean*: proverbial in English, but here attested for the first time. Aristotle and his followers, the Peripatetic school, argued that virtue came between two extremes.

XI

1 *Quinctius*: nothing is known for certain about this Quinctius, but a C. Quinctius was patron of the town of Aeclanum in the territory of the Hirpini in central Italy in 85 BC.

17 See introductory note to I. xviii.

XII

A *recusatio* (see note on I. vi). Here Horace starts with a snatch in the grand style, declines to write praise of the wars of Augustus, suggests that Maecenas should do it in prose, and ends with a demonstration of his own love poetry.

1   *Numantia*: city in northern Spain inland of the Cantabri (see II. xi. 2).

2   *purpled with Punic*: with a play of words. The Latin word *Poenus* means Carthaginian (Carthage, in North Africa, was a colony of the Phoenician city of Tyre). *Poeniceus* means purple (from the dye of the *murex* shellfish, processed in Phoenicia). Rome won great sea battles against the Carthaginians at Mylae in 260 BC and the Aegatian Islands in 241 BC. Again at Mylae Octavian's fleet under Agrippa defeated Sextus Pompeius in 36 BC.

5   *Hylaeus*: a Centaur who fought against the Lapiths. See note on I. xviii. 7.

7   *sons of earth*: an allusion to the battle of the gods and the Giants, in which Hercules assisted the gods.

XIII

8   *Colchian poisons*: Colchis was the home of Medea. See notes on *Epodes* iii. 9–14 and v. 21–4.

15 *Bosphorus*: the Straits were dangerous to shipping and the sailor who negotiated them might well be tempted to relax his vigilance.

24–6 *Sappho . . . Alcaeus*: see Introduction, page xv.

33 *the hundred-headed*: Cerberus, the dog that guards the kingdom of Pluto in the Underworld, has fifty heads in Hesiod, *Theogony* 312, but normally has only three. The variant is chosen no doubt because it adds to the surrealistic piquancy of this passage (30–6) by inviting us to calculate how many ears Cerberus lays upon the ground as he is put to sleep by Alcaeus' lyre.

37–9 *Prometheus . . . Pelops . . . Orion*: here inhabitants of the Underworld, although Prometheus is normally pecked by the eagle on a cliff in the Caucasus. The father of Pelops is Tantalus (*Epode* xvii. 67). For the sin of Orion, the great hunter, see III. iv. 70–2.

XIV

7–8 *Tityos . . . Geryon*: Tityos was one of the sons of earth (II. xii. 7), whose body covered 9 acres in the Underworld. Geryon was a Spanish monster with three heads.

17–19 *Cocytus . . . Danaus . . . Sisyphus*: Cocytus was a river of the Underworld. Forty-nine of the fifty daughters of Danaus murdered their bridegrooms on the marriage night and were condemned to spend eternity trying to fill a cistern with leaking jars (see notes on III. xi. 24 and 35). For Sisyphus see *Epode* xvii. 67–8.

XV

3   *Lucrine*: a lake near Puteoli, famous for the huge engineering feat which linked it with Lake Avernus to form the *Portus Iulius*, as a harbour for Octavian's navy in the war against Sextus Pompeius in 37–36 BC.

5   *elm*: vines were married to elms and poplars.

11   *Romulus . . . Cato*: both famous for frugality. Romulus was believed to have limited land-holdings to 2 acres, and Cato was the archetypal Sabine peasant, opposed to all forms of luxury.

17   *turf*: traditionally used for simple country buildings. Augustus himself lived simply, but boasted that he found Rome brick and left it marble.

XVI

7   *Grosphus*: Pompeius Grosphus, a prosperous Sicilian landowner (see lines 33–4 and *Epistles* I. xii. 22).

9   *lictor*: an attendant who cleared a path for Roman magistrates with his rod.

17   *javelins*: grosphos is the Greek for a throwing spear.

22   *squadrons*: Horace is conjuring up the spectacle of the Roman Knights, *Equites*, in their parade splendour (see note on III. i. 40).

39   *a Greek Camena*: Camena is the *Latin* Muse. Horace is playing with his claim to have naturalized Greek poetry in Latin (see III. xxx. 13–4).

XVII

19   *horoscope*: Maecenas appears to have been interested in astrology (see 22–3). Horace here is alluding to different forms of horoscope.

25   *theatre*: see note on I. xx. 3.

XVIII

6   *Attalus*: see note on I. i. 13.

14   *one and only*: this seems to mean a) that the Sabine country is uniquely wonderful, and b) that the Sabine estate is all he wants (see note on I. xx. 1).

21   *Baiae*: fashionable seaside resort on the bay of Naples.

36   *steward of Orcus*: the steward of the god of the Underworld is the god Mercury, responsible for the shepherding of the dead (see I. x. 17–20).

37–8 *Tantalus*: one of the sinners suffering eternal punishment in the Underworld (see *Epode* xvii. 64–5). His descendants include some of the leading figures in Greek epic and tragedy, Pelops and his sons Atreus and Thyestes (see note on *Epode* v. 86), Agamemnon and Menelaus, sons of Atreus, and Aegisthus, son of Thyestes.

XIX

8–9 *thyrsus . . . Thyiades*: the Thyiades, Maenads, devotees of Bacchus, who carried the thyrsus, the Bacchic wand tipped with pine cones, ivy, or vine leaves, at whose touch milk and wine burst from the earth, and honey oozed from tree trunks. Horace may yet again, as at I. xvii. 22, be playing with etymology (the Greek *thuo* means 'I rave').

14   *blessed wife*: Ariadne, abandoned by Theseus on the island of Naxos, and loved by Bacchus.

15   *Pentheus*: king of Thrace whose palace as well as his body were torn to pieces for opposing Bacchic rites.

16   *Lycurgus*: another king of Thrace cruelly punished for his opposition to the rites of Bacchus.

19   *Bistonian women*: Thracian Bacchants.

23   *Rhoetus*: another Giant (see note on II. xiv. 7).

29–32 *golden horn . . . tongues*: Bacchus is sometimes seen as a bull. Here the heads of Cerberus are reduced to three (contrast II. xiii. 33), setting us another arithmetical problem in fitting tongues to feet and legs. The allusion is to the descent of Bacchus into the Underworld to rescue his mother Semele.

XX

1   *flimsy*: the word *tenuis*, 'fine' is the hallmark of the refined, low-key Hellenistic poetry of Callimachus, which Horace has claimed to be reproducing (see note on I. xxxi. 16). In the envoi to this book, he suggests that he is also aiming higher, but does so with some self-mockery. Hence the translation of *tenuis* as 'flimsy'.

13   *Icarus*: see note on I. iii. 34. Continuing the self-mockery, Horace compares himself not with Daedalus who flew, but with Icarus who fell.

15–18 *Syrtes . . . Hyperborean . . . Geloni*: the Syrtes are sands on the north coast of Libya. The Hyperboreans add the north to the other cardinal points in this passage. The Geloni are a Scythian people. Praise of Augustus' conquests often boxes the compass. Here the fame of Augustus' poet does so also.

20 *Rhône-swigger*: in poetry the inhabitants of a place are sometimes referred to by naming the river they drink. Here the Rhône-dwellers are said to drink deep of their river (see note on I. xviii. 9).

24 *empty*: the mock-pomposity of this grand finale ends with a pun. The honours would be empty, that is needless, useless. So would the tomb of Horace. The swan has flown.

ODES, BOOK III

The first six odes in this third book are commonly known as the Roman Odes. They are the only series of six odes in the same metre, the only series of six long odes, and the only series of six odes on political subjects.

I

1–4 In this preamble to the Roman Odes the priest of the Muses is clearing the sacred area before he speaks to the young. Augustus laid great stress upon the importance of moulding the minds of the young.

1 *profane*: literally 'in front of the shrine' (*fanum* is a shrine).

8 *his eyebrow*: Homer's Zeus requires both at *Iliad* i. 528.

10 *Campus*: elections were held on the Campus Martius. The ferocity of political ambition had been a feature of the civil strife that had marked the last century of the Republic. In the Augustan settlement the elections were controlled by the *Princeps*.

16 *urn*: in II. iii. 25–8 when your lot is shaken out, you die.

17 *naked sword*: Damocles envied the lot of Dionysius king of Syracuse and was invited to sit in the tyrant's chair at dinner on the following evening. Above his head a naked sword hung by a hair.

20 *birds*: caged birds were sometimes kept to sing the wealthy to sleep.

23 *Tempe*: the Thessalian beauty spot stands here for any lovely, wooded valley.

27–8 *Bear . . . Kid*: the Bear is the constellation Arcturus. The Kid alludes to the constellation of the Haedi. Storms are frequent at the setting of the first and the rising of the second. Latin poets enjoy the surreal effect of imagining the constellations as animals.

33   *piers*: wealthy Romans loved to build out over the sea. Many fine
     examples are depicted in Pompeian paintings.

40   *Knight*: the *travectio*, the annual parade and inspection of the
     Equestrian Order, the Knights (as at II. xvi. 22), renewed and
     assiduously practised by Augustus. This was 'a noble sight and
     worthy of the greatness of the Roman Empire' (Dionysius of
     Halicarnassus VI. xiii. 4). No doubt some of these wealthy owners
     of coastal villas would have maintained bronze-plated triremes as
     pleasure cruisers.

43   *Sidon*: a city in Phoenicia which produced purple dye.

44   *Achaemenids*: the proverbially wealthy Persian dynasty. 'Oil of
     balsam is by far the most valuable of all oils' (Pliny, *Natural History*
     xxiii. 92).

45   *entrance hall*: ostentatious building was a fashion among the rich,
     and particular extravagance was lavished on doors and doorposts
     (see note on *Epode* ii. 7).

47-8 *Why should I . . . labour*: it is no accident that the opening of this
     series of political odes should state a personal viewpoint. A key part
     of the Augustan programme was that it claimed to offer civilized
     freedom to individuals after the breakdown of law and order of the
     previous century.

II

15   *hamstrings*: Roman soldiers were trained to cut the hamstrings of
     fleeing enemies.

17   *the polls*: for elections see note on III. i. 10.

19   *axes*: carried by the consul's attendants to symbolize his right to
     inflict capital punishment.

23   *dank earth*: Stoics believed that on death the souls of the virtuous
     rose to coalesce with the divine fire surrounding the universe.

25   *faithful silence*: Romans valued a friend who could respect a confi-
     dence. The *Apophthegmata* of Augustus collected by Plutarch in-
     form us that Augustus once quoted Simonides, fragment 528: 'For
     silence, too, there is a secure reward.'

27   *the Mysteries of Ceres*: Augustus was an initiate and took the rites
     seriously (Suetonius, *Life* 93).

III

9-15 In this list of heroes Pollux, brother of Castor, was son of Jupiter
     and the mortal Leda. He was a benefactor of mankind in storms at

sea (see note on I. iii. 1–4) and in battle (I. xii. 21–2). Hercules, son of Jupiter and the mortal Alcmena, was a benefactor of mankind by his labours in many countries to rid the world of monsters. Augustus, the central of these five figures, was the adopted son of Julius Caesar, deified after his assassination, and Horace is here tactfully prophesying what everyone knew, that Augustus too would be deified after death. His lips will then be stained with purple as he drinks the nectar. Bacchus, son of Jupiter and the mortal Semele, benefactor of mankind for his invention of wine, is often portrayed in Greek art in a chariot drawn by tigers. Romulus, founder of Rome, was son of Mars and the mortal Ilia, the Trojan priestess of line 33. A different version of his ascension is alluded to at I. ii. 47.

19–20 *judge . . . woman*: oracular reference to Paris of Troy (Ilium), and Helen, wife of Menelaus, king of Sparta (see line 25 and note on I. xv. 1–2).

21 *Laomedon*: king of Troy, father of Priam. He commissioned Apollo and Neptune to build walls for his city and refused to pay them the promised reward. Virgil sees this deceit as an ancestral guilt of the Trojans/Romans which has brought upon them the curse of civil war (*Georgics* i. 502).

32 *grandson*: Juno was the wife (and sister) of Jupiter (line 64); Mars the son of Jupiter; and Romulus the son of Mars.

46 *the middle sea*: the Mediterranean parts Europe from Africa at Gibraltar and at the Bosphorus. This survey of the Augustan Empire looks east, south, and north (see note on II. xx. 16).

58 *on condition*: there is no record under Augustus of any intention to move the capital to the site of Troy. The best sense that can be made of this passage is that the Augustan picture of the war against Antony and Cleopatra was of a clash between the forces of the barbarous East and the civilized West, a picture made plausible by the Donations of Alexandria in 34 BC, whereby Antony made over Egypt, Cyprus, and all Roman territories in Asia to Cleopatra and her children. On this interpretation the ode is not advice to Augustus, but condemnation of Antony.

IV

1 *Calliope*: 'noblest of the Muses' (Hesiod, *Theogony* 79), later responsible for epic poetry. The pipe (2) suggests choral lyric, the lyre and cithara (4) would then suggest solo song (see note on I. i. 33–4).

6-7 *madness . . . groves*: divine madness seizes the tender virgin soul in
Plato, *Phaedrus* 245, and the Muses have gardens and groves and
fountains in Plato, *Ion* 534.

9-24 *Apulian Vultur . . . Baiae*: after the intensely Greek opening
Horace moves to his birthplace in south Italy and, without expect-
ing to be taken literally, claims for himself a poetic myth like the
stories which gathered round the names of Greek poets. When
Stesichorus, for example, was a baby, a nightingale perched on his
lips and sang (Pliny, *Natural History*, x. 82). The place-names in
lines 14-16, which would have been obscure to a contemporary
Roman, further make the point, that Horace is doing for Italy what
the great lyric poets had done for Greece. The invocation of the
Camenae (21), the Muses of Italy, is a resounding statement of that
claim.

20 *filled*: we think of inspiration as god breathing into man, but in this
Platonic context (see note on 6-7 above) we should rather see the
god as being inside the man. According to Plato, *Phaedrus* 533 E-
534 E, the poet is *entheos*, he no longer has his own mind or spirit
or breath (*anima*). He is full of the god, as Horace is at II. xix. 6 and
III. xxv. 2. Here then, literally, Horace was 'an infant *with anima* not
without the gods', *non sine dis animosus infans*. And Latin speakers
would have enjoyed the literal meaning of 'infant'. Horace could
not yet speak.

26-8 Here Horace suggests that the Muses saved his life at the battle of
Philippi (II. vii. 1-14); when the tree fell on his estate (II. xiii. 1-12);
and on some voyage on the west coast of Italy round Cape
Palinurus south of the bay of Naples, where Aeneas' pilot of that
name was lost overboard in *Aeneid* v. 859.

34-5 *Concanians . . . Geloni*: tribes in north-west Spain and in Scythia.

38-40 *cohorts . . . Pierian cave*: from the Suetonian *Life of Virgil* 27, we
know that Virgil read the *Georgics* to Augustus as he was recovering
from a sore throat. At this time a pressing problem for Augustus
was the demobilization of the huge armies he had mustered for the
war against Antony and Cleopatra. His *Res Gestae* iii and xxviii
show that he took pride in solving it.

43-4 *Titans . . . thunderbolt*: the war between Jupiter and the Titans is
an analogy for the war between Augustus and Antony.

70-80 *Orion . . . Tityos . . . Pirithous*: all guilty of sexual sins. Tityos
was killed by Apollo and Diana for his attentions to their mother
Latona, and punished by daily visits of the vulture to his ever-
renewing liver, the seat of sexual desire. Pirithous descended to

Hades in an attempt to ravish its queen, Proserpina. A key feature of the Augustan presentation of the war with Antony and Cleopatra was the condemnation of the sexual pleasures in which they indulged.

V

In 53 BC a Roman army under Crassus was defeated by the Parthians at Carrhae. This ode might be seen as opposition to a proposal that the prisoners of war taken at Carrhae should be ransomed. This does not make satisfactory sense. Since men under arms in 53 BC would not be likely fighting material in the twenties, the arguments of lines 25–32 would be on this interpretation irrelevant. It is far more likely that the poem is rather a general endorsement of Augustan policy to glorify the idealized republican virtues and use the legendary republican heroes like Regulus as examples to urge moral virtues upon young Romans in Augustan Rome.

13 *Regulus*: Roman general captured in the first Punic War. In 255 BC he was sent back to Rome to sue for peace and an exchange of prisoners, but instead argued against the proposal.

55–6 *Venafrum . . . Tarentum*: see II. vi. 11–22.

VI

3 *the crumbling temples*: (in 28 BC) 'I restored 82 temples in the city, neglecting none which at that time required to be restored.' This is Augustus' claim in his *Res Gestae* xx. It would be naïve to suppose that here, in a poem published five years after the event, Horace is truly advising Augustus to adopt this policy. It is sound tactics for the client to 'advise' the patron to do what his patron has already done.

9 *Monaeses . . . Pacorus*: Parthian leaders. Pacorus defeated a Roman army under Antony's general Decidius Saxa in 41 BC. Monaeses was engaged in the vigorous Parthian resistance to Antony's invasion of Parthia in 36 BC.

45–8 This bleak end to the Roman Odes must surely be read with an if-clause understood. In 18 BC the Julian Laws were to be passed regulating marital behaviour. In 23 we may guess that Augustus' intentions were known, and opposition expected. Horace is here giving warning that decadence will follow *if* Augustus' reforms are not implemented.

VII

5   *Gyges*: a Greek name, but his exercises on the Campus Martius tell us that we are to think of him as a Roman (see note on I. viii. 2).

the She-goat: Capra, or Capella, a star in Auriga. Its rising was at the end of September. See note on III. i. 27–8.

6   *Oricum*: a port in a north-facing bay on the north-west coast of Greece, into which Gyges has taken shelter from the fierce south winds of winter. Since it is almost due east of Brindisi, which would be Gyges' landfall in Italy, the western breezes of line 2 will not blow him home, but they will mark the coming of spring and the season of navigation, and he will manage to tack into them.

14–17   *Proetus . . . Peleus*: Proetus was the husband of Stheneboea, who was enamoured of their guest Bellerophon. When Bellerophon refused her, she persuaded her husband to try to have him killed, by claiming that Bellerophon had attempted to seduce her. A similar story is told of Hippolyte, wife of Acastus, and their guest Peleus. Although line 9 speaks simply of Gyges' hostess or land-lady, *hospita*, it is an obvious guess that she is the wife of his host in Oricum. The go-between is spinning the tale, by saying that Bellerophon was *too* chaste, and by glozing over the fact that Bellerophon escaped the attempt on his life.

18   *resisting Hippolyte of Magnes*: a town in Thessaly, famous for the attracting stone, the *magnes* found there. Peleus resisted the attraction. Horace enjoys such word play with Greek. Similarly, Asterie is presumably as lovely as a star (Greek *aster*); Gyges, king of Lydia, was proverbially wealthy; Chloe (10) is jealous, *Chloe* in Greek is a green shoot and in a famous poem (fragment 31), Sappho was greener than grass (Greek *chloe*) when she saw her beloved with a man; Enipeus was plaintive, and *eniptein* is the Greek verb 'to scold'.

VIII

1   *first of March*: Mothers' Day.

3   *living turf*: hints that Maecenas is visiting Horace on his Sabine farm.

5   *dialogues*: Some fragments survive of Maecenas' *Dialogi* (see note on III. xxi. 7).

12   Lucius Volcacius Tullus was consul in 66 BC and had a son of the same name who was consul in 33 BC. Horace likes to choose a meaningful vintage. If it is the older Tullus, he may be imagining

the scene as taking place in 26 BC, and so choosing a forty-year-old wine. If it is the younger Tullus, perhaps 33 BC was the year Horace received the Sabine farm and had this escape from death. This ode, appearing in 23 BC, would then be humorously commemorating Maecenas' gift ten years before.

IX

There are several indications that we are meant to suppose that the male speaker is Horace: Lydia's fame (7) might come from her association with a poet; she seems to have moved on to a younger lover (16), a pattern which has already discomfited Horace at I. v. 1 and xiii. 11; the speaker is said to be fickle and quick-tempered (22), both failings which Horace elsewhere admits (fickleness frequently, quick temper at *Epistles* I. xx. 25); and, last and most telling, again and again he is defeated in this war of words.

7–8 *Lydia . . . Ilia*: the name Lydia would suggest that the lady was of Lydian extraction and was therefore rich (see note on III. xvi. 41). But Ilia caps it (see note on I. ii. 15–18).

9–13 *Thracian . . . Thurii*: a Thracian slave girl or freedwoman would not be of high social standing, and if a slave she would have no legal parents. Thurii, on the other hand, was a Greek colony built on the site of the ancient and famous city of Sybaris in south Italy. Sybaris was proverbially rich and luxurious. Calais was clearly a free citizen with a father, Ornytus, both of them names of heroes who had sailed with Jason to capture the Golden Fleece.

X

1 *drinking . . . the distant Don*: therefore a South Russian (see note on II. xx. 20).

5–6 *trees . . . courtyard*: this sounds like the house of a wealthy Roman with its enclosed garden.

11–12 *Etruscan . . . suitors*: some Etruscans, like Maecenas, achieved wealth and eminence in Augustan Rome and lived in great luxury. Penelope, wife of Odysseus, was the exemplar of marital fidelity.

XI

1 *Mercury*: god of many functions, including persuasion (I. xxx). He taught Amphion to move stones with his lyre-playing in order to build the city of Thebes.

5   *dumb and graceless*: as the tortoise would have been before Mercury strung its shell with sheep gut (see note on I. x. 6).

13–24 The focus shifts slightly, from the lyre to its great executant Orpheus, and in particular to his visit to the Underworld in a vain attempt to bring his wife Eurydice back to life.

24 *daughters of Danaus*: Danaus agreed to give his fifty daughters in marriage to the fifty sons of his enemy, and instructed them to murder their bridegrooms on the wedding night. One of the great showpieces of the Augustan reconstruction of Rome was the fifty reliefs depicting this episode in the portico of the temple of Apollo on the Palatine, dedicated in 28 BC. This statuary receives direct praise from Propertius at II. xxxi. 4. Virgil gives the tale a conspicuous and subtle role in the *Aeneid* (x. 497–9 and xii. 941–4). This acknowledgement by Horace of the Augustan monument is the most idiosyncratic.

35 *whose name*: Hypermestra is so famous that her name does not have to be mentioned.

XII

4   *Cytherea*: a title of Venus, mother of Cupid. She had a shrine on the Aegean island of Cythera.

8   *Bellerophon*: Hebrus must have been quite a rider. Bellerophon rode the winged horse Pegasus.

XIII

This is a hymn, an act of worship to a fountain or to the divinity Horace perceives in it. We recognize the hymn form because of the invocation, the name of the cult site, the praise of the deity (all in the first line), the description of the ritual (lines 2–8), the previous services of the god (lines 9–12), the repeated occurrences of the second person. See note on I. ii. 26–52. Country piety goes with loving observation of country matters—the shining water, the weary oxen, the cattle standing in the water, the dark evergreen overhanging the bright spring, and the personification of the waters as busy, chattering women.

3   *a kid*: the worshipper loves the victim, and is moved by the details of the rite, as he imagines the (hot) red blood staining (and warming) the cold (clear) water. The date is 12 October, the day before the *Fontinalia*, when the spring kids were being weaned and their horns beginning to show.

13 *a famous fountain*: like the fountains of the Muses in Greece. Horace is claiming that his Italian Bandusia will be ranked with

Castalia, Hippocrene, Pirene, and Aganippe (see note on III. xxx.
13–14). He states his claim with a touch of Greek syntax, literally
'You too will become of the famous fountains'.

XIV

3   *returns . . . from Spain*: this is a formal welcome for Augustus on his
return from his campaign against the Cantabri. He was expected
home in the autumn of 25 BC, but was delayed by illness. Now in
the spring of 24 he comes in triumph from Spain, just as Hercules
had done after slaying Geryon, as celebrated, also in an Augustan
connection, by Virgil in *Aeneid* viii. 184–365.

6   *come forth*: when a general returned to Rome to celebrate a triumph
he was required to spend one night outside the city walls, and his
family (here his wife Livia and his sister Octavia), friends, and the
Senate would be among those who came in solemn procession, to
greet him and to thank the gods for the fulfilment of their prayers
for his safety.

9   *maidens*: these would be the maidens who in the previous year (see
note on line 3) had welcomed the young men home from the war in
Spain.

10–11 *boys and . . . girls*: children attended such sacred ceremonies, as
for instance in the depiction of Augustus' family on the Ara Pacis.
All the more necessary to stress the importance of ritual silence (III.
i. 2).

18–20 *Marsian war . . . Spartacus*: in 91–88 BC Rome fought the Social
War against the peoples of Italy, including the Marsi. In 73 she
quelled the slaves' rising led by Spartacus. Horace thinks of a fifty-
year-old vintage, partly because to Roman taste it would have been
delicious, partly because of its historical associations. Fifty years
ago nothing was safe; now, with the defeat of the Cantabri,
Augustus governs a settled and secure world.

28   *Plancus*: another meaningful vintage. In 42 BC, when Plancus was
consul and Horace fought against Octavian at Philippi, Horace's
disputes and quarrels were not all amorous.

XV

14   *Luceria*: in Apulia, 70 km. north-west of Horace's birthplace,
Venusia.

XVI

Critics dislike this poem. The key to understanding it is the first poem
in Book I, addressed to Horace's patron Maecenas, as is the last in

Book II. Horace loves variety and, besides, he has other plans for the first and last places in Book III. The first poem in the second half of Book I (I. xx) is a poem of subtle praise and gratitude to Maecenas, spiced with a declaration of independence. So too here, the poem that begins the second half of the book is a subtle poem of gratitude and praise, with a declaration of independence, addressed to Maecenas. When Horace speaks to his patron, we have to be on the lookout for humour. This ode begins with the lofty mythological exemplum of the rape of Danaë by Jupiter, taking the form of a shower of gold. The first stanza rolls formally along, every noun with its adjective falling pat, but our antennae twitch at the word 'enough' and at the description of Jupiter Best and Greatest as an adulterer who comes by night. In the second the word 'frightened' reminds us neatly of the story. Acrisius locked up his daughter Danaë because he had been told in a prophecy that he would be killed by her son. The humour bursts out at the divine metamorphosis when the god becomes the fee. By so drastically rationalizing the myth, Horace is having one of his many digs at fashionable philosophy.

3   *fortified*: a military metaphor flickers throughout the first 24 lines of the poem.

11   *lightning*: Epicureans believed that lightning could go through stone walls and split towers open (Lucretius vi. 229, 240). The common notion was that Jupiter wielded it, but in this instance he clearly judged that gold would be more effective.

12   *the augur of Argos*: Eriphyle was bribed by the offer of a gold necklace to persuade her husband Amphiaraus, priest king of Argos, to go to war against Thebes. He did as she wished although he foresaw that it would mean his death. In due course the necklace brought death also to Eriphyle, to her son Alcmaeon, and to all who owned it. Amphiaraus himself was literally overwhelmed (13), buried alive, in the retreat from Thebes.

13   *the hero of Macedon*: sarcastic reference to Philip who had said that any citadel could be taken if an ass with a load of gold could climb up into it.

16   *sea captains*: perhaps Menas, freedman of the Pompeys, is included, who changed sides repeatedly, doing brilliant service in sea battles between Sextus Pompeius and Octavian, till he was killed by the Siscians in 35 BC. A fair guess would be that he was hanged from his own yard-arm.

18–20   *lift up my head . . . Knights*: oblique praise of Maecenas for refusing to become a senator (as at I. xx. 5 and Propertius III. ix. 21).

25–38 These stanzas express Horace's gratitude for the small Sabine estate he received from Maecenas. For the stream (29) see praise of Bandusia at III. xiii. For woodland see I. xxii. 10. He is confident in his harvests, because his needs are small, and he is not a commercial graingrower or a producer of vintage wines. Laestrygonian casks would hold the great wines produced round Formiae, as in I. xx. 9–12 (Formiae was thought to be the Laestrygonia which Odysseus called at in *Odyssey* x. 80–133).

38 *you would not refuse*: Horace is often chastised for revealing here that his poverty is unreal. He has taken that risk in order to make it clear that he knows that Maecenas would be endlessly generous, and that he himself does not want any more than he has already received. He is quietly asserting his independence, as he has already done with a touch of humour at lines 22–4.

41 *Alyattes*: father of Croesus and king of Lydia, an ancient empire famous for its wealth. Phrygia was an extensive neighbouring kingdom and Roman landowners were very eager to possess their neighbours' estates (see note on II. ii. 11).

XVII

Mock-pedantic praise of the ancient family of Aelius Lamia and an ideal picture of a wealthy Roman in his villa, with his slaves enjoying an enforced holiday because of bad weather.

1 *Lamus*: king of the Laestrygonians (see note on xvi. 25–38 above). His kingdom was thought to be near Formiae, on the coast some 110 km. south of Rome, where the Lamiae family had an estate. The prodigious, long sentence and the fact that the Laestrygonians were cannibals are part of the ponderous genealogical joke.

7–8 *Liris . . . Marica*: the River Liris wended its way through marshes to the sea at Minturnae, where the goddess Marica was worshipped.

15 *Genius*: the divine spirit within all of us. It enjoys wine and the other pleasures of life.

XVIII

Horace promises to respect the festival of Faunus on 5 December, the Nones, if Faunus will not molest the young of his flocks. He then modulates to a description of his farm on the holy day of the god.

1   *Faunus*: the Italian god of the countryside, equated with the Greek Pan, who is interested also in nymphs, wine, wolves, and dancing (see lines 1, 6–7, 13, 15, and I, xvii).

13   *the wolf ambles*: from the jokes in lines 1 and 7, this is a cheerful poem, and here in high spirits Horace claims a Golden Age miracle for his own country festival.

14   *foliage*: The path of a god was often strewn with leaves or flowers (e.g. Lucretius ii. 627–8). Here Horace pretends that December's fallen leaves are a tribute to the god.

XIX

After a dinner celebrating the appointment of Murena as augur, Horace rounds on an antiquarian bore and calls for wine, music, and love. Those who revere the Graces will mix three ladles of wine with nine of water. The poet will invert the ratio.

1–4   *Inachus ... Codrus ... Aeacus*: Inachus was the founder king of Argos; Codrus the last king of Athens at the end of the eleventh century BC who gave his life in battle to secure victory against Dorian invaders; Aeacus was the father of Peleus and Telamon. Telamon himself, his two sons Teucer and Ajax, and Achilles, son of Peleus, all took part in expeditions against Troy.

8   *Paelignian cold*: On a cold evening in Rome Horace thinks of the east wind blowing from the mountains of the Paeligni to his Sabine farm, and thence to Rome.

18   *Berecyntian*: see note on I. xviii. 14.

26   *the Evening Star*: Venus.

27   *Rhode*: Lycus is an old neighbour with a young wife. Rhode and Telephus are young, Horace and Glycera not so young. Perhaps Rhode is the wife of old Lycus.

28   *roasting*: for the cooking metaphor see note on I. xiii. 8.

XX

15   *Nireus*: much of the fun in this poem is the application of epic elements to a less than epic episode. It ends with Nireus, 'the loveliest of the Greeks who went to Troy' (*Iliad* ii. 673) and Ganymede, the Trojan shepherd and prince, snatched from his flocks on Mount Ida to be the cupbearer of Jupiter. Homer's 'many-fountained Ida' has become, mischievously, 'well-watered'.

XXI

A parody of a hymn, addressed to a jar of wine, with many of the hymn features noted on I. ii. 26–40 and in the introduction to III. xiii.

1   *Manlius*: see note on *Epode* xiii. 6.

7   *Corvinus*: Marcus Valerius Corvinus Messalla was given a part in one of the *Dialogi* of Maecenas along with Virgil and Horace (see note on III. viii. 5). A surviving fragment of this work, entitled 'On the Power of Wine', attributes to Corvinus the observation that 'it makes one's eyes easily seducible' (cf. line 21), 'makes everything more beautiful and brings back the pleasures of youth'. This mention of Corvinus' interest in wine is therefore an elegant compliment to Maecenas.

11 *Cato*: Censor in 184 BC, whose strict morality did not exclude the convivial pleasures.

14 *Lyaeus*: title of Bacchus, from the Greek *luein* 'to loosen', as in *Epode* ix. 38.

XXII

1   *Virgin*: Diana was goddess of women, childbirth, the moon, and, as Hecate, the Underworld. Her festival was on 15 August.

5   *my villa*: yet another delicate statement of gratitude to Maecenas who gave it.

XXIV

2   *untouched*: Augustus tried to get his hands on them in 26–25 BC (see note on I. xxix 2–3).

28 *Father of Cities*: Caesar was hailed as Father of the City, *Pater Urbis*, just before his death. Augustus was to take the title in 2 BC.

34 *punish vice*: in 18 BC, five years after these poems appeared, Augustan legislation, the Julian Laws, attempted to reward marriage and deter sexual licence. This poem therefore supports views which were later to emerge as law, and must have been forming in Augustus' mind and conversation for several years. Maecenas and Augustus were in close contact in the early twenties and Maecenas and Horace were friends. Horace is surely not *advising* Augustus, but Augustus would have been pleased to read the views expressed in this poem (see note on III. vi. 45–8).

47   *Capitol*: Augustus (perhaps in 28 BC) dedicated 16,000 pounds of
      gold, and pearls and other jewellery to the value of 50 million
      sesterces in the temple of Jupiter on the Capitol (Suetonius, *Life of
      Augustus* 30).

XXV

A hymn in praise of Bacchus, Augustus, and poetry. See II. xxix.

9-11 *Bacchant*: the orgiastic cult of Dionysus (in Latin Bacchus), was
      associated with Thracian women. Hebrus is a Thracian river and
      Bacchants would worship at night on the Thracian mountains, one
      of which was Mount Rhodope.

18   *Lenaeus*: a cult title, *lenos*, in Greek, being the vat in which the
      grapes were trodden.

XXVI

10   *Memphis . . . Sithonian*: Memphis was a shrine of Venus, just south
      of the Nile delta. The Sithonian peninsula in Thrace is the middle
      of the three which jut south into the north Aegean.

XXVII

Horace wishes Galatea a safe journey, warns her of the dangers of
seafaring, but consoles her, not too seriously, by the example of the sea
trip of Europa, the daughter of Agonor, king of Tyre, who was seduced
by Jupiter in the form of a bull, and carried across the sea to Crete.

1   *omens*: augury is the art of divination from the flight of birds.

1-16 In the opening of this poem with its zoo of nine animals and its
      pretentious language Horace is making fun of the augural arts
      (compare his mockery of genealogy at the opening of III. xvii and
      antiquarianism at the opening of III. xix). This is confirmed by a
      deliberate obfuscation in the mumbo-jumbo. On the one hand,
      since Lanuvium in line 3 lies just south of Rome to the west of the
      Appian Way, the four omens for enemies in the first stanza would
      therefore all be coming from the traveller's *right*, the *unfavourable*
      side according to Roman augury. Similarly in line 10 Horace is
      summoning a raven from the *left*, the east, as a *favourable* sign for
      Galatea. On the other hand, in lines 15 and 16 Horace the augur
      calls for magpie and woodpecker as *unfavourable* signs from the
      left. He seems to be having fun with the technicality that some
      birds are favourable on the left and others on the right (Plautus,
      Asinaria 260).

14 *remember me*: Horace is fond of Galatea. The analogy with the myth of Jupiter and Europa suggests that she is leaving him to go with a new lover. He wishes her happiness, and assures her that it is possible for her to find it.

34–66 Europa's utterance shows at several points that she is an unusually silly girl.

42 *Gate of Ivory*: in Homer, *Odyssey* xix. 560–7 Penelope tells Odysseus that the dreams which come to us through the Gate of Horn are true, and those which come through the Gate of Ivory are false.

72 *horns to rend*: Venus is making fun of Galatea's bluster in lines 46–8.

73–6 the implied analogy between Galatea's lover and Jupiter adds to the humour of the piece.

XXVIII

2–7 *action . . . fast*: military metaphor. Wisdom is the fortress. Caecuban wine is the artillery to use against it. Time is another enemy and his ranks are giving way, not standing fast. Lyde's bombardment with Caecuban must show him no mercy.

8 *Bibulus*: consul with Caesar in 59 BC, known as the consulship of Julius and Caesar because Bibulus tried to block Caesar's legislation by absenting himself from the Senate to watch the sky for omens. The amphora is delaying because Bibulus delayed. It is delaying also because Bibulus is bibulous and wants to keep it for himself.

12 *Cynthia*: Diana, goddess of women (see on III. xxii. 1).

14–16 the last love poem in Horace's revolutionary collection of lyric poems ends with Venus, not named, but alluded to evocatively with reference to her shrines in the Greek islands. Its last note is a note of sadness. *Odes* I. v was a farewell to elegiac love; III. xxviii is a farewell to love.

XXIX

6–8 *Tibur . . . Aefulae . . . Telegonus*: Tibur (see note on I. vii. 13), Aefula, and Tusculum, which was founded by Telegonus, who unwittingly killed his own father Odysseus, are three towns on the hills within 30 km of Rome, visible from the tower Maecenas built in his garden on the Esquiline.

17–19 *Andromeda ... Procyon ... Leo*: Cepheus is a constellation and
    father of Andromeda; Canis Minor is the lesser Dog-star, Procyon
    (in Greek 'Pre-dog'). It is the beginning of the Dog-days in Au-
    gust. Maecenas would enjoy the play with the stars (see notes on II.
    xvii. 19 and III. i. 27–8).

35 *the Tuscan sea*: the Tiber is the Tuscan river, and flows into the
    Tuscan sea, that is the Tyrrhenian Sea west of Rome. This is
    relevant to the Etruscan origins of Maecenas alluded to in the first
    line of the poem (see note on I. xx. 6).

63 *two-oared*: the point is that one man can row it.

XXX

7   *Libitina*: the Roman goddess of funerals.

9   *priest*: the *Pontifex Maximus* led solemn processions which in-
    cluded the Vestal Virgins up the Sacred Way to the Temple of
    Jupiter Best and Greatest on the Capitol. Horace underestimated.

11 *Daunus*: legendary founder king of Daunia, the ancient kingdom in
    which Venusia, Horace's birthplace, was situated. The River
    Aufidus flowed close to Venusia, in winter and spring a torrent, but
    not in summer.

13 *bring*: the Latin word *deduxisse* is used of establishing a colony; also
    of spinning wool. It is a standard claim of Hellenistic poets (and the
    Latin poets they inspired) that their verse is fine-spun (see on I.
    xxxi. 16 and II. xx. 1).

13–14 *Aeolian ... Italian*: his proudest boast (see notes on I. xxxii. 3, II.
    xvi. 39, III. iv. 9–24 and xiii. 13).

15 *well-deserved*: with characterisitic evasiveness Horace leaves the
    reader to decide whether it is Melpomene who deserves the honour
    or Horace.

15–16 *Melpomene ... Delphi*: invoked at the end of the first poem in the
    three books, and thanked at the end of the last as Horace claims the
    laurel crown of Apollo, god of poetry.

SECULAR HYMN

In 23 BC Horace produced his three books of Odes, a collection of daring
and original poems by which he hoped to be acclaimed as the lyric poet
of Latin, worthy to be ranked beside the great lyric poets of Greece. In
this hope he felt somewhat disappointed (see *Odes* IV. iii. 15–16), and his
next work, the first book of *Epistles* in 19 BC, was a collection of verse

letters, equally subtle and original, but in much more conversational language. In that same year occurred the death of his friend Virgil, author of the *Aeneid*, Rome's greatest epic, and generally hailed as the greatest of the Roman poets. In 18 BC the Julian Laws were passed to regulate marriage and the procreation of children and the year 17 BC was selected to celebrate the achievements of the Augustan regime, including this reform of Roman morals. This Secular Festival, the first since 146 BC, was named from the Latin *saeclum*, a century or a generation, on the understanding that nobody who had been alive on a previous festival could still be alive during the next. In September 1890, while digging on the banks of the Tiber on the site of the Festival, a workman came across a large marble inscription, most accessibly described in E. C. Wickham's commentary on the Hymns (Oxford, 1896). This inscription, freely used in the notes below, gave a detailed account of the Augustan Secular Festival, ending with the words *carmen composuit Quintus Horatius Flaccus*, and the hymn which Horace composed was this *Carmen Saeculare*.

The Festival was spread over three nights and three days from the first to the third of June 17 BC. According to the inscription the goddesses to whom prayers were offered on these nights were the Fates, the Parcae of line 25, Ilithyia, goddess of childbirth (line 13), and Mother Earth (line 29). Prayers were offered to Jupiter on the first day, and he enters the Festival Hymn at line 31, and is clearly included in the great invocation to the gods which begins in the central stanza of the Hymn at line 37. This tacit understanding is made explicit at line 50, since the inscription tells us that on the first day Augustus and Agrippa each sacrificed a male ox to Jupiter, and each sacrificed two female oxen on the second. On the third day they offered holy cakes to Apollo and Diana, and Horace's Secular Hymn was performed before the Temple of Apollo on the Palatine and then again on the Capitol.

The Secular Hymn has not pleased Latin scholars. Some eminent Horatians confess that they have never been able to read it through. In this they are like contemporary musicians, concert promoters, and radio producers, who fail to allow for facts which Horace firmly grasped, that sung words are almost entirely indistinguishable to almost all listeners, and that the more voices in a choir the more indistinguishable they are. If, in addition to these handicaps the voices are sopranos, like the fifty-four singers in Horace's choir, and if they are singing unamplified before a large audience in the open air, the difficulty is compounded. Wagner knew this, and wisely buried his orchestra in a covered hole between singers and audience. Horace, too, knew it, and composed the expected message in expected terms, with only small variations on established forms. So, for instance, the Julian marriage laws *Leges De*

Maritandis Ordinibus appear in line 19 as *lege marita*, and the list of Augustan slogans in lines 57–60 would have come winging to the ears of the expectant multitude. This is not a Horatian Ode with rich overtones of allusion and intriguing modulations of tone and pace. It is broad-brush poster art for a state occasion, and demonstrates the flexible intelligence of its creator.

1   *Phoebus and Diana*: on the third evening of the Festival, Augustus and Agrippa prayed to these two gods, and then 27 boys and 27 girls whose parents were still alive sang this Festival Hymn, first on the Palatine and then on the Capitol. Phoebus Apollo and his sister Diana are eternally young, and therefore predominate in this Hymn. The young singers start with them, renew the invocation just before the middle of the poem where the rest of the great Roman gods are addressed, and address them again in the last four stanzas.

5   *Sibylline verses*: these prophecies were in the care of a board of men, the Fifteen, who used them to authenticate the date and format chosen for the festival. The relevant Greek text is preserved in Zosimus ii. 6.

9   *gleaming chariot*: the performance on the Palatine would have taken place within sight of the golden statue of the chariot of the Sun on the roof of the Temple of Palatine Apollo.

13 *Ilithyia*: Augustus prayed to this Greek goddess of childbirth on the second night of the Festival. Here (after lines 1 and 9) she is apparently seen as one of the manifestations of the Roman goddess Diana.

19 *marriage law*: the Julian Laws of 18 BC were celebrated in this Festival and in this Hymn. It was largely a women's festival, as can be seen from repeated emphases throughout and in the choice of goddesses to whom prayers were made on its three nights, the Fates, Ilithyia, and Mother Earth.

22 *games*: as held in the theatre and the Circus for a week after the formal ritual.

24 *glad nights*: traditionally this festival was dedicated to gods of the Underworld. This Augustan celebration pointedly ignores them. Hence the sacrifice of white oxen (50). Offerings to the Underworld gods would have been black.

25 *Parcae*: the Latin inscription, being adapted from the Greek Sibylline verses (see note above on 5), gives them their Greek name, *Moerae*, the Fates.

30   *Ceres*: during the famine of 22 BC the people of Rome prevailed
     upon Augustus to take over responsibility for the corn supply (Dio
     Cassius liv. 1).

37-52   An extended tribute to Virgil's *Aeneid* ending with a clear
        echo of one of its most famous lines, where Anchises advises
        the Romans 'to spare the defeated and war down the proud' (vi.
        853).

49-50   *blood of Anchises ... white oxen*: Augustus, descendant of
        Aeneas, son of Venus and Anchises, sacrificed a white ox to Jupiter
        and Juno at the Festival. The absence of the name of Augustus
        makes the praise more tactful and more effective.

54   *Alban axes*: the kings of Alba Longa were the descendants of
     Aeneas and the ancestors of Augustus.

56   *audience*: literally 'responses'. In his *Res Gestae* xxxi, Augustus
     proudly records the names of peoples who sent embassies to him to
     request the friendship of the Roman people.

65   *altars*: of the glorious Augustan temple of Apollo on the Palatine,
     before which was given the first performance of this Hymn.

70   *the Fifteen*: see note above on line 5.

ODES, BOOK IV

I

In this love poem Horace tells Venus he is too old for love. It is a
variation on the *recusatio* (see note on I. vi).

9-10   *liver to roast*: for the liver as the seat of sexual desire, and for
       smiling allusion to sexual desire in a cooking metaphor, see note on
       III. xix. 28.

12   Paulus Fabius Maximus was consul in 11 BC, two years after this
     ode was published, and thereafter had a distinguished career, and
     become a trusted friend of Augustus. But that was all in the future.
     The two puzzles of this ode are that such a young, unproven man
     should be in a position of such prominence at the opening of the
     book and that he should be praised in terms of his future success in
     love. One other item of evidence may help to solve these problems.
     At some stage in his life Paulus married Augustus' cousin Marcia
     and the wedding may have occurred between the writing of this
     ode and Paulus' consulship two years later. This conjecture solves
     both problems and makes sense of the middle of the poem as a

tribute to a wealthy, young man, owner of a glorious villa in the Alban hills, who was about to marry into the imperial family.

II

1   *Iullus Antonius*: born in 44 or 43 BC, son of Antony and his first wife Fulvia, brought up by his second wife Octavia, sister of Augustus, married Octavia's daughter Marcella in 21 BC, aedile 16 BC, praetor 13 BC, and consul 10 BC.

Pindar: (518–438 BC) poet of Thebes, of which city Dirce (25) was the fountain. He wrote in metres Romans did not understand (7, 12), a great variety of poems including dithyrambs in praise of Dionysus (11); paeans and hymns in praise of gods and heroes (13); odes for victors in the games, including the Olympian Games held at Elis in Olympia (19) and Pythian Games at the shrine of Apollo at Delphi (9); and dirges, *threnoi* (21–4). Horace declines, in a fair Latinization of the Pindaric manner, to rival Pindar.

3   *Daedalus*: see note on I. iii. 34.

28   *Matine*: the Matine shore was in South Italy, near Horace's birthplace Venusia. He contrasts his modest origins with the glories of Theban Dirce.

30   *Tibur*: see note on I. vii. 13. Horace here belittles his own work, but hints that it has the Callimachean virtues of brevity, learning, discrimination, and carefulness.

33   *Iullus*: wrote an epic poem on the exploits of Diomede. Horace here, as in IV. i, is ringing the changes on the *recusatio*, and contriving to praise both Augustus and Iullus in one ode. The end of the poem praises the poetic gifts of Iullus by suggesting that in comparison Horace will be an ordinary Roman citizen shouting sincere and artless praise in the street.

34   *the Sugambri*: in the summer of 16 BC this tribe crossed the Rhine and defeated M. Lollius, proconsul of Gaul, capturing a legionary standard. When Augustus left Rome to engage them they immediately withdrew and sued for peace. Augustus then stayed away from Rome till July 13 BC organizing the administration of Gaul and Spain. The dramatic date of this ode is perhaps 14 BC, when Rome is preparing for his return. In fact Augustus refused the triumph which Horace here so vividly imagines, even to his own humble part in it, joining the citizens on the pavement in the rhythmic chants (47–8) with which triumphant generals were traditionally greeted.

42 *the Forum*: on days of festival the legal business of the Forum was suspended.

54 *a tender calf*: the offering from Horace is properly modest, but the sacrificer chooses the victim with tender, loving care (III. xiii. 3–8).

III

The first six lines look to Greece, to the Isthmian and other victory odes of Pindar. Lines 7–9 look to Rome, to the triumphing general who defeats kings, the abomination of the Romans. In the third stanza Horace makes his own claim as the man who has brought Greek lyric poetry to Rome (see note III. xxx. 13–14). The Greek poets pleased the cities of Greece; Horace pleases the chief of cities. In lines 15–16 he reveals that he had been disappointed with the reception of the first three books of the *Odes* in 23 BC but reassured by the recognition he received in being invited to compose the Secular Hymn in 17 BC. In lines 16–20 he veers away from any expression of pride in this achievement, by rising as though into the hymn style (see note on I. ii. 26–52), and giving all the credit for his fame to the Muse.

IV

This ode celebrates the victory in 15 BC of Nero Claudius Drusus (born 38 BC) and Tiberius Claudius Nero (born 42 BC) over the Vindelici, a people on the north side of the Alps. Drusus and Tiberius were the sons of Livia and her first husband, also called Tiberius Claudius Nero. After Augustus had divorced his first wife, 'because he was heartily sick of her shrewishness', as he himself said, he at once took Livia Drusilla away from her husband although she was pregnant at the time, and 'he loved and cherished her alone his whole life long' (Suetonius, *Life of Augustus* 62). He also adopted her two sons, Hence the climactic introduction of the word *Nerones* at the end of the first huge sentence (line 28) and the mention of the Claudians at the end of the ode. After declaring in IV. ii the folly of any attempt to rival Pindar, he now in IV. iv writes an ode in the style of Pindar's victory odes. The daring simile with which the ode begins, the majestic opening sentence, and the detailed picture of the eagle are all declarations of Pindaric intent: see *Olympian* vii and *Pythian* iv and i.

1   The lightning-bearer was sent to abduct the cupbearer.

6–10 *long since . . . then . . . soon . . . and now*: the eagle's life has four phases. Latin similes tend to correspond at many points with the narrative. So here we may remember the death of Drusus' father *long since* in 33 BC when he was 5 years old, *then* his quaestorship in 18 BC, *soon* his easy victory over the Raeti, *and now* his substantial conquest of the Vindelici in 15 BC, both of them largely pastoral peoples (10, 15). Compare Cassius Dio liv. 22: 'The Raetians, who inhabit a territory between Noricum and Gaul north of the Alps, were overrunning a large part of Gaul . . . and carrying off plunder even from Italy . . . Because of these outrages, then, Augustus *first* dispatched Drusus against them. He *soon* routed a body of Raetians which had advanced to meet him . . . Some while later Augustus also sent out Tiberius. Both commanders *then* invaded Rhaetia' and fought a victorious campaign from Gaul to the Danube. In this ode Horace gives greater credit to Drusus than to Tiberius. Augustus would have approved.

18–22 The parenthesis on local practices, and the refusal to speak further, are both Pindaric. See *Isthmian* i. 63 and *Olympian* i. 30.

25–8 Augustus paid great attention to the upbringing of members of his family. He taught his grandsons Gaius and Lucius to read, to swim, and to write the same hand as his own. He made a point of seating them beside him when they dined in his company, and being alongside them when they travelled together (Suetonius, *Life of Augustus* 64). No doubt he took equal care of his stepsons Drusus and Tiberius.

29–32 *brave . . . dove*: Horace alludes to the word *nero* which in Sabine means brave and strenuous in war. The aphorism (*gnome* in Greek) linking blocks of sense, is Pindaric (see *Olympian* xii. 7–12). So too is the animal analogy as in 'The red fox and the roaring lion cannot change the nature born in them' (*Olympian* xi. 19–21).

33 *yet training*: this calculated rejection of Pindar's insistence on the paramount importance of breeding is a compliment to Augustus' care for his stepsons.

38 *Metaurus*: in 206 BC, during Hannibal's invasion of Italy in the Second Punic War, when Hasdrubal was hoping to join forces with him in central Italy, he was defeated and killed in a battle near the River Metaurus in Umbria, in which the consul C. Claudius Nero played a distinguished part.

39 *bright day*: days of good omen were marked white on the Roman calendar.

51 *the richest triumph*: the Latin is *opimus triumphus*, literally 'a fat triumph'. There was no such thing but the phrase hints at the *spolia opima*, awarded to any Roman commander who killed the leader of the enemy forces in single combat. It may also hint at

the scant flesh the Carthaginians are likely to eat in this contest of deer with wolves.

50–76 Hannibal does not speak in character as a Carthaginian. Lines 53–6 allude to the story of Virgil's *Aeneid*, in which Aeneas rescues the gods of Troy, his son, and his father from the burning city; lines 61–4 exploit Greek mythology in Hercules' fights with the Hydra, the water-snake of the Lernaean Marsh, and also in the crops of warriors sown and instantly grown in Colchis against Jason and in Thebes against Cadmus; lastly, the eloquent praise of the Claudians is impressive but surprising on the lips of their enemy.

V

1–8 In June 16 BC, just before Augustus went to deal with the Sugambri in Gaul (see note on IV. ii. 34), he dedicated the Temple of Quirinus (Romulus). He did not return till July 13 BC. Ennius (*Annales* 105–9) celebrated an earlier member of the Julian family in similar terms:

> . . . longing possesses their hearts and they say
> to each other 'Romulus, Romulus, *divinely* radiant,
> what a guardian of our homeland the *gods* have borne
> in you! O Father, O begetter, O blood sprung from the *gods*,
> you have given us birth into the shores of light!

Ennius states the divinity of Romulus three times. Horace instead states the goodness of Augustus three times in his first two stanzas and once in the last. Public worship of Augustus was not encouraged in Rome during his lifetime, but see lines 33–6.

5 *leader*: Latin *dux*, had military associations in the Republic. Here *dux bone*, 'good leader' is a demilitarized adaptation.

9–24 The long sentence about the desolate mother in lines 9–16 throws into relief the regularity of what follows. Lines 17–24 convey the inventory of benefits conferred by Augustus in a style which suggests the epigrammatic bareness of a Roman inscription.

17–20 Augustan peace, settled agriculture, and prosperity are seen as important elements of the Augustan achievement, for example in art, particularly the Ara Pacis Augusti, erected to celebrate his return in 13 BC. The God of Plenty, Faustitas, implying divinely blessed prosperity, occurs only here in surviving Latin. Since the defeat of Sextus Pompeius in 36 BC the sea had been clear of piracy.

21–4 *debauchery*: the Julian Laws (supported by Horace in III. vi. 45–8, passed in 18 BC, and celebrated in the Secular Hymn) strengthened penalties for adultery and offered rewards for childbearing.

25–8 In 20 BC Augustus had retrieved the standards captured by the Parthians in 53 BC. Probably about the same time the Scythians sent an embassy to Rome, the Vindelici in Germany were subdued in 15 BC, and Augustus spent most of 14 BC in completing the pacification of Spain.

32 *the second course*: although worship of Augustus was discouraged in Italy, after the capture of Alexandria in 30 BC it was decreed that a libation should be poured to him at every banquet private or public. He was clearly destined to become a god and the poets sometimes anticipate destiny.

37–40 *Hesperia*: the land of the west, particularly Italy. This panegyric of the public achievements of Augustus ends, as does III. xiv, with a cheerful personal celebration. It is as though Horace judges the work of a political leader by the happiness of those he leads, and as though his drinking corresponds to the nightly bath of the sun.

VI

This ode is addressed to Phoebus Apollo as god of poetry. Hence the allusion to Niobe who boasted that she had twelve children while Latona had only two, Diana and Apollo. These two killed her twelve. Hence too Tityos, killed by Apollo and Diana while trying to ravish their mother. The tone is heightened by the huge opening sentence and the postponement of Apollo's name till line 25.

3–24 *Achilles . . . auspices*: the pivot on which the ode turns from Greece to Rome. If Achilles had lived, no Trojans would have survived the sack of the city and Rome would not have been built.

22–3 *your words . . . Venus . . . walls*: a tribute to the epic by Horace's friend Virgil. In *Aeneid* iii Apollo's words guided the Trojans on their wanderings; at i. 229–53 Venus appealed to Jupiter on behalf of her son Aeneas; and the poem opens by announcing that the sufferings of Aeneas are the origin of the lofty walls of Rome.

28 *Smooth-cheeked Agyieus*: Phoebus Apollo as god of streets and doorways, the most learned and exotic of the five Greek words which in lines 25–8 convey the glories of Greek poetry. The glory is continued in Latin by the poet from the town of Venusia in Daunia (see notes on III. xxx. 13–14 and IV. ii. 28), who writes with

the breath of the Greek god Phoebus within him (see note on III. iv. 20). The growing of the beard and the cutting of the hair (see IV. x) are the beginning of manhood for the Roman. Apollo is eternally young. Hence his hair is never cut and his chin never knows a beard.

25–44 The reference to Apollo's eternal youth leads to the address to the young in lines 31–2 and the reference to the Secular Hymn. We have seen in IV. iii. 13–16 how Horace viewed his appointment to compose the Hymn as the supreme recognition of his life's work. Here the allusions are more detailed: the boys and girls had to be the children of noble Roman families with their mothers and fathers still alive; the stress in the Festival was upon women, marriage, and childbirth, in accord with the provisions of the Julian Laws of 18 BC; and most of these last fourteen lines of this ode are specifically devoted to girls and women.

36 *my thumb*: Horace pictures himself directing the choir of 27 girls and 27 boys from the lyre and presumably he did so for the performance on the third day of the celebrations. That does not mean that the great poet of Rome trained the choir. In the last words of the poem he is careful not to say so.

38–42 *Noctiluca . . . lights*: 'the Night-shiner' is a unique title of Diana as goddess of the moon, alluding to the fact that this was partly a night festival; in line 39 the allusion to agricultural prosperity comes within Diana's province and is a recurrent Augustan theme; and the lights of line 42 remind the audience that all free persons were given torches with which to illumine the night rituals.

VII

A. E. Housman found this the most beautiful poem in the Latin language. This may be partly because from the first words 'fled are the snows' it repeatedly alludes to change and the rapidity of change, perhaps nine times in the first thirteen lines.

15 *Aeneas . . . Tullus . . . Ancus*: Aeneas was famous for his piety, Tullus, the third king of Rome, for the enlargement of the power and wealth of the city, Ancus, the fourth, for his goodness.

21–2 *Minos . . . splendid*: the shining son of Zeus held a golden sceptre as he administered justice to the dead in Homer *Odyssey* xi. 568–9.

23 *ancestry . . . eloquence*: Manlius Torquatus was a member of a distinguished Roman family, whose work as a barrister is repeatedly alluded to playfully in *Epistles* I. v.

25-8 *Hippolytus . . . Pirithous*: Hippolytus died preserving his chastity against the addresses of his stepmother Phaedra, but the goddess of chastity does not rescue him from the Underworld. Pirithous was captured in an attempt to ravish Persephone, the queen of the Underworld. Theseus had accompanied him, and returned later to the Underworld with Hercules, but he could not release his beloved Pirithous and bring him back to the upper world.

VIII

4 *Censorinus*: Horace looked upon the commission to compose the Secular Hymn as the culmination of his career as a poet (see IV. iii. 13-16 and vi. 25-44). In IV. ix he writes a defence of the career of Lollius, who was a member of the committee responsible for the Secular Festival. Here in IV. viii when he addresses to a Censorinus this poem on the importance of poetry, this is surely not the young Censorinus, but Lucius Marcus Censorinus, who was one of the two senators who tried to defend Julius Caesar on the Ides of March in 44 BC, and who, crucially, was also involved in organizing the Secular Festival for 17 BC.

6 *Scopas . . . Parrhasius*: the message is serious, but the tone is humorous. Masterpieces by the sculptor Scopas or the painter Parrhasius working at the end of the fifth century BC and the first half of the fourth, were for the extremely wealthy, and Horace mocks Parrhasius in lines 7 and 10, remembering that the painter called himself a *bon viveur*, a *habrodiaetus*. Horace compliments Censorinus by saying that he is not interested in such luxuries. From line 13 onwards the ode is a stout assertion of the *value* of poetry and is replete with commercial terms, as in lines 1, 5, 10, 12, 19, 22. In 27 the Isles of the Blest are called in the Latin 'the *Wealthy* Isles' and in 29 the Muse literally '*enriches* with the sky'.

17 This line cannot be by Horace. The number of lines in every ode of Horace except this one is divisible by four. The references to the defeat of Hannibal, to the winning of the name Africanus (in 19-20), and to the work of the poet Ennius from Rudiae in Calabria, point clearly to Ennius' patron Scipio Africanus Maior and the taking of Carthage in 202 BC, not to Scipio Africanus Minor who destroyed it in 146 BC. The removal of line 17 would reduce the number of lines in the poem to 33. To reduce it to 32, the prime suspect is line 33, four words in Latin of which three are repeated from III. xxv. 20. Nowhere else in the *Odes* does such a degree of repetition occur. The removal of the line produces a low-key ending which surprises, but is not un-Horatian.

26   *Aeacus*: Greek hero, then Judge of the Dead, frequently praised by Pindar.

29   *Hercules*: see note on III. iii. 9–15.

34   *Bacchus*: the name of the god refers to his gift. The end of the poem looks back to the beginning in that the word for 'friends', *sodales*, suggests 'drinking companions'. The suggestion may be that Censorinus and Horace consulted each other in convivial circumstances in planning Horace's contribution to the Secular Festival.

IX

1–12   *Lest you should suppose . . . Aeolia*: the solemn opening raises the Italian peasant, born near the far-sounding Apulian River Aufidus, to join the company of such famous Greek poets as Homer the Maeonian, Simonides of Ceos, and Sappho from the Aeolian island of Lesbos.

17–19   *Teucer . . . Idomeneus and Sthenelus*: Greeks who besieged Troy under Agamemnon in Homer's *Iliad*.

21–2   *Hector and bold Deiphobus*: Trojans, ancestors of the Romans, are not forgotten.

31–52   *Lollius . . . homeland*: consul 21 BC and one of the committee of fifteen who had organized the Secular Festival of 17 BC and presumably commissioned Horace to compose the Secular Hymn. Compare Censorinus in the previous ode. In 16 BC as proconsul in Gaul he was defeated by the Sugambri and lost a legionary eagle. This incident became known as the Lollian disaster, *clades Lolliana*, but Augustus continued to use him for a series of important administrative assignments. The last two stanzas are a massive attempt to vindicate his reputation. Horace praises Lollius for his non-military virtues, his industry, wisdom, judgement, and incorruptibility, and daringly deploys military language in lines 43–4, and again in 51–2. Here it is implied that the *clades Lolliana* was no disgrace, and in the last two lines Horace speaks of him in the same terms as he has already applied in line 24 to the Trojan/Roman heroes.

X

3   *the feather*: an astonishing metaphor, apparently referring to the first down on the boy's chin (see note on IV.vi. 28).

XI

1-12 In earlier invitation poems Horace has stressed the simplicity of his provisions. Here, on the other hand, there is a catalogue of luxuries, all expressed in monotonously regular Latin to give the impression that Horace is sparing no expense.

19 The name of Maecenas had appeared in Horace's earliest work and in 19 BC at the beginning of the first book of the *Epistles* Horace had promised it would appear in his last. Here in pride of place in the centre of the poem, Horace restates his affection for his patron and friend with a characteristically intimate allusion. Maecenas was of Etruscan stock and would have acknowledged with a smile the Etruscan etymology of the word for the Ides, the day which *splits* the month of April (line 15) on the thirteenth. In Etruscan the verb *iduare* means to divide.

21-36 *Telephus*: It seems strange to woo a woman by hinting that she is too old for the man she really loves, who is besides already in thrall to a rich young woman. Perhaps there is another aspect to Horace's tactic here. All of the non-political poems in this book are concerned with the passage of time, the irrevocability of the past. Horace is telling Phyllis that they are both old and subject to those laws. Love no longer offers them the supreme joys they knew in their youth. The boastful opening might then be read as self-mockery. Here is the wealthy poet who has everything except youth. He has already had trouble with a young Telephus at I. xiii. 11.

XII

1 *the Thracian winds*: spring winds normally blow from the west; Thracian winds would be northerlies. Presumably the Thracian winds that come with the spring are unlike the northerlies of winter.

6-7 *Itys . . . Cecrops*: Procne, of the house of Cecrops, king of Athens, punished her husband Tereus, king of Thrace, for ravishing her sister Philomela, by serving him the flesh of their son Itys. Procne was changed into a swallow, Philomela into a nightingale, and they were both pursued by Tereus, now a hoopoe. T. S. Eliot in *The Waste Land* has 'The change of Philomel, by the barbarous king | So rudely forced . . . | and still she cried, and still the world pursues'.

14-16 *Virgil . . . young nobility*: in the works of Horace the word must refer to his friend, generally held to be the greatest of the Roman poets, but he had been dead for six years by the time this book was published in 13 BC. Either this is an ode Horace rescued from a drawer (we know from *Ars Poetica* 388 that he approved of putting poems away in drawers) to evoke the golden past when they were both young, making their way, and enjoying badinage with each other and with such noble patrons as Octavian and Maecenas, both about half a dozen years younger than Virgil; or else Horace wrote the ode specially for this collection as an evocation of the distant past. In either case it would fit the mood of the two poems which precede it in this collection. The tone of the letters of Augustus quoted in the Suetonian *Life of Horace* shows that the teasing of young Virgil for his mercenary attitude need not be shocking or tasteless. Besides, such jokes, along with protestations of poverty from the young host, are common enough in invitation poems (see Catullus 13).

XIV

7–16 *Vindelici . . . Raeti*: see note on IV. iv. 6–10.

10–11 *Breuni . . . Genauni*: neighbours of the Vindelici.

29 *Claudius*: here Tiberius. See note on IV. iv. 6–10.

35 *Alexandria*: The defeat of the Vindelici in 15 BC was fifteen years after the conquest of Alexandria in 30 BC (I. xxxvii. 25).

42–50 *Cantabrian . . . Sugambri*: this summary of Augustan conquests resembles his own claims in *Res Gestae* xxxvi–xxxiii.

XV

This poem includes an inventory of Augustan motifs: in line 5 agricultural prosperity as at IV. v. 17–8; in lines 6–8 the recovery of the standards as at *Res Gestae* xxix; in lines 8–9 the closing of the Gates of War as in *Res Gestae* xiii; in lines 10–11 and 27 the Julian Laws of 18 BC as in the Festival Hymn; in line 12 the resuscitation of republican ideals as for example in I. xii. 37–44, III. v, and III. vi. 33–44; in lines 13–16 and 21–4 the celebration of world conquest (see note on II. xx. 16); in lines 17–20 the end of the Civil Wars and the creation of Augustan Peace, the *Pax Augusta*, as for example at II. i. 29–36 and III. xiv. 14–16; in line 28 the religious revival and the near deification of Augustus, as for example at III. v. 1–4, III. vi. 1–4, and IV. v. 32; in lines 31–2 the praise of Augustus by praise of Aeneas and the Julian family, as in Virgil's *Aeneid*.

29–32 It was a traditional Roman practice to sing the praises of noble ancestors at the end of family suppers. Here Horace proposes that this practice should be continued, but suggests that if his own odes, like these celebrating members of the Julian family, are sung, the Roman tradition will be strengthened by the influence of Greek (Lydian) poetry which he brought to Italy. In the last lines of all he touches a note often struck in this fourth book, an allusion to the masterpiece of his friend Virgil, who had died six years before these poems appeared.

GLOSSARY

Acheruntia town near Horace's birthplace VENUSIA

Achilles son of Peleus and the goddess Thetis, greatest warrior of the Greeks at the siege of Troy

Aeacus judge of the dead, in his lifetime king of Aegina, and famous for his piety

Aeolia area on the northern seaboard of Asia Minor including Lesbos, home of Sappho and Alcaeus

Alban Ascanius, son of Aeneas, founded the city of Alba Longa and the dynasty of the Alban kings

Anacreon (born *c.*570 BC) Greek poet famous for poems of love and wine

Antiochus III (*c.*242–187 BC) king of Syria, fought against the Romans *c.*189 BC

Aphrodite in Latin Venus

Apollo see under PHOEBUS

Archilochus (late 8th or early 7th cent. BC) Greek iambic and elegiac poet

Augustus (63 BC–AD 14) see under OCTAVIAN and Introduction, pages xii–xxi

Bacchus god of wine. See introduction to I. xviii. 1

Bactria modern Afghanistan

Baiae fashionable seaside resort on the Bay of Naples

Bandusia fountain, probably on Horace's Sabine estate

Bantine woods high woods south-east of Venusia

Berecyntian of Mount Berecyntus in Phrygia, see note on I. xviii. 14

Caecuban famous Campanian wine

Calenian famous Campanian wine

Callimachus (*c.*305–*c.*240 BC) Alexandrian poet. See note on II. xx. 1

Calliope see under MUSES

Camenae the Latin Muses

Cantabrians people in north-west Spain, repeatedly at war with Rome till subjugated by Agrippa in 20 BC

Caria country in the south-west corner of Asia Minor

Carthage great North African city against which Rome fought three Punic wars: the first (264–242 BC), the second (218–202 BC) in which Hannibal invaded Italy, and the third (151–146 BC) which ended with the capture and destruction of the city

Cato the Elder (234–149 BC) strict guardian of Roman traditions

Cato the Younger (95–46 BC) archetypal republican who committed suicide rather than live under Julius Caesar

Centaurs half-men half-horses. See note on I. xviii. 7

Chimaera monster with a lion's head, a snake's tail, and its own body

Clio see under MUSES

Cnidos island south-west of Asia Minor famous for its shrine of Aphrodite

Colchis on the eastern shore of the Black Sea, home of the sorceress Medea. See note on *Epode* V. 21–4

Cotiso Dacian leader

Cyclades islands to the east of the Peloponnese

Cyclopes blacksmiths in the forges of VULCAN

Cyprus the island of Aphrodite

Cythera island off the south coast of the Peloponnese, birthplace of Aphrodite

Dacia province on the north of the Danube at war with Rome 29–28 BC

Danaus instructed his fifty daughters to murder their bridegrooms, sons of his brother Aegyptus

Diana goddess of women, childbirth, the moon, and, as Hecate, of the Underworld

Dio Cassius (consul AD 205 and 229), author of a Roman history written in Greek

Dionysus the Greek Bacchus

Elis plain in the north-west of the Peloponnese. The Eleans presided over the Olympian Games

Erato see under MUSES

Euterpe see under MUSES

Falernian famous wine from south Latium

Faunus god of the forests, in Greek Pan

Forentum town south of VENUSIA

Formian famous wine from south Latium

Gaetulia a country to the south of MAURETANIA

Garganus mountainous promontory forming a spur above the heel of Italy

Getae Thracian tribe on the lower Danube

Gyges hundred-handed Giant

Hannibal great Carthaginian general who invaded Italy in the Second Punic War (218–201 BC)

Hector greatest of the Trojan warriors

Hesperia the land of the west, an ancient name for Italy. From the point of view of Rome it could refer to Spain

Hipponax (mid-6th cent. BC) Greek iambic poet

Iapyx west-north-west wind

Indians sent several embassies to Augustus

Ixion attempted to ravish Hera and endured eternal torment in the Underworld

Jove see under JUPITER

Julian Laws enacted in 18 BC to regulate marriage and the procreation of children

Juno sister and wife of Jupiter, in Greek Hera

Jupiter in Greek Zeus, king of the gods

Lapiths a Thessalian tribe famous for its battle with the CENTAURS. See note on I. xviii. 7

Lares the dead ancestors, gods of the family

Liber another name of Bacchus, god of wine

Lipara largest of the Aeolian Islands north of Sicily

Liris river flowing between south Latium and north Campania, among the great Caecuban, Calenian, Falernian, and Formian vineyards

Lydia country on the western seaboard of Asia Minor, just north of Caria

Maecenas (c.70–8 BC) chief minister of Octavian/Augustus till early in the twenties, patron and friend of Horace

Maenad ecstatic female worshipper of Bacchus

Maeonia area in central Asia Minor, leading claimant as birthplace of Homer

Mars god of war, father of Romulus and Remus

Marsians warlike people in central Italy, east of Rome, traditional allies of Rome

Mauretania country stretching along the western shore of North Africa

Medes see under PERSIANS

Melpomene see under MUSES

Mercury messenger of the gods, in Greek Hermes. See note on I. xxx. 8

Minerva the Latin PALLAS ATHENA

Minos judge of the dead, in his lifetime king of Crete

Muses daughters of Jupiter and Mnemosyne, the goddess of Memory. The nine Muses are Calliope, their leader, the Muse associated with epic, Clio with history, Euterpe with the music of the pipe, Terpsichore with lyric poetry (dance), Erato with lyric poetry (love poetry and hymns), Melpomene with tragedy, Thalia with comedy,

Polyhymnia with mime, and Urania with astronomy. This allocation of separate provinces to the Muses was not firmly established in Horace's time, and the invocation of the Muse can stand as the invocation of them all

Niphates range of mountains in Armenia

Octavian Gaius Octavius, great-nephew of Julius Caesar, adopted as Gaius Julius Caesar Octavianus, took the name Augustus in 27 BC

Orcus another name for PLUTO, god of the Underworld

Orion name of a mighty hunter and of a constellation which rises in storm in March and sets in storm in November

Pactolus gold-bearing Lydian river

Pallas Athena Greek warrior goddess, patroness of arts and crafts, in Latin Minerva

Paphos shrine of Aphrodite on the west coast of Cyprus

Parthia country to the south-east of the Caspian Sea. The Parthians defeated a Roman army under Crassus at Carrhae in 53 BC. Their horsemen were famous for the Parthian shot, an arrow delivered in retreat

Patareus port on the south coast of Lycia, famous for its temple of Apollo

Penates gods of the store cupboard, the chief private cult of every Roman household

Persia in Horace's day part of the Parthian empire, and in itself no threat to Rome. Horace refers to the Parthians as Persians or Medes to suggest that Rome's wars with the Parthians made them successors to the Greeks who defended Western civilization against the Persians in the 5th cent. BC

Philippi (42 BC) battle in which Antony and Octavian defeated Brutus and Cassius, the assassins of Julius Caesar

Phoebus Apollo eternally youthful god of archery, music, medicine, prophecy, and the arts of civilization. See note on I. xxxi. 1

Pieria district of Macedonia on the northern slopes of Mount Olympus, home of the Muses

Pindar Greek poet (518–438 BC), famous for his choral odes. See Introduction pages xiv, xv, xxi and note on IV. ii. 1

Pliny the Elder (AD 23/4–79) author of a 'Natural History', a universal encyclopedia in thirty-seven books

Pluto god of the Underworld

Polyhymnia see under MUSES

Praeneste ancient Etruscan city east of Rome, modern Palestrina

Priam king of Troy

Proserpina queen of the Underworld

Punic Wars see under CARTHAGE

Pyrrhus (319–272 BC) king of Epirus in north-west Greece, fought against the Romans in 280–275 BC

Quirinus another name for Romulus

Res Gestae Divi Augusti the formal record of the achievements of Augustus, set up as an inscription at his death in AD 14

Romulus founder of Rome. See note on III iii. 15

Sabines a people in the Apennine mountains, taken to represent all the country virtues

Salii priests of Mars famous for their dancing in triple time and their lavish feasts

Scythians inhabitants of a country on the north shore of the Black Sea, who sent an embassy to Augustus in 25 BC

Semele mother of Bacchus

Silvanus god of the countryside

Simonides (*c*.556–468 BC) Greek elegiac and lyric poet from Ceos

Social War fought between Rome and her allies (*socii*) in Italy (91–88 BC)

Stesichorus Greek lyric poet of the first half of the 6th cent. BC

Styx a river of the Underworld

Syrtes dangerous sands on the north coast of Africa, now on the gulfs of Gabas and Sirte

Tarentum port founded by Sparta, in the Tarentine Gulf, the arch of the foot of Italy

Tempe beautiful valley in Thessaly

Terpsichore see under MUSES

Thalia see under MUSES

Tibur town in the hills east of Rome, a popular resort of wealthy Romans

Troilus youngest son of PRIAM, killed by Achilles

Urania see under MUSES

Ulixes Latin form of the name Odysseus

Venafrum mountain town in the Samnite country, east-south-east of Rome

Venus the goddess of love, mother of Aeneas, whose son Iulus gave his name to the Julian family. Augustus, adopted son of Julius Caesar, was a Julian

Venusia Horace's birthplace in northern Apulia in south Italy. See Introduction pages viii–x

Vesta the Roman goddess of the hearth, served by the Vestal Virgins

Vulcan husband of Venus and god of fire, who supervised the Cyclopes in their task of making the thunderbolts under the volcanic mountains of south Italy and Sicily

Vultur a mountain visible from Horace's home town VENUSIA

INDEX TO LATIN TITLES

The Oxford World's Classics Website

www.worldsclassics.co.uk

- Browse the full range of Oxford World's Classics online

- Sign up for our monthly e-alert to receive information on new titles

- Read extracts from the Introductions

- Listen to our editors and translators talk about the world's greatest literature with our Oxford World's Classics audio guides

- Join the conversation, follow us on Twitter at OWC_Oxford

- Teachers and lecturers can order inspection copies quickly and simply via our website

www.worldsclassics.co.uk

American Literature

British and Irish Literature

Children's Literature

Classics and Ancient Literature

Colonial Literature

Eastern Literature

European Literature

Gothic Literature

History

Medieval Literature

Oxford English Drama

Poetry

Philosophy

Politics

Religion

The Oxford Shakespeare

A complete list of Oxford World's Classics, including Authors in Context, Oxford English Drama, and the Oxford Shakespeare, is available in the UK from the Marketing Services Department, Oxford University Press, Great Clarendon Street, Oxford OX2 6DP, or visit the website at www.oup.com/uk/worldsclassics.

In the USA, visit www.oup.com/us/owc for a complete title list.

Oxford World's Classics are available from all good bookshops. In case of difficulty, customers in the UK should contact Oxford University Press Bookshop, 116 High Street, Oxford OX1 4BR.